Four Corners

Jack C. Richards · David Bohlke

1A

Student's Book

CAMBRIDGE UNIVERSITY PRESS
Cambridge, New York, Melbourne, Madrid, Cape Town, Singapore,
São Paulo, Delhi, Dubai, Tokyo, Mexico City

Cambridge University Press
32 Avenue of the Americas, New York, NY 10013-2473, USA

www.cambridge.org
Information on this title: www.cambridge.org/9780521126571

First published 2012

Printed in Hong Kong, China, by Golden Cup Printing Company Limited

A catalog record for this publication is available from the British Library.

ISBN 978-0-521-12657-1 Student's Book 1A with Self-study CD-ROM
ISBN 978-0-521-12660-1 Student's Book 1B with Self-study CD-ROM
ISBN 978-0-521-12649-6 Workbook 1A
ISBN 978-0-521-12652-6 Workbook 1B
ISBN 978-0-521-12646-5 Teacher's Edition 1 with Assessment Audio CD / CD-ROM
ISBN 978-0-521-12640-3 Class Audio CDs 1
ISBN 978-0-521-12619-9 Classware 1
ISBN 978-0-521-12638-0 DVD 1

For a full list of components, visit www.cambridge.org/fourcorners

Cambridge University Press has no responsibility for the persistence or
accuracy of URLs for external or third-party Internet Web sites referred to in
this publication, and does not guarantee that any content on such Web sites is,
or will remain, accurate or appropriate. Information regarding prices, travel
timetables, and other factual information given in this work are correct at
the time of first printing, but Cambridge University Press does not guarantee
the accuracy of such information thereafter.

Art direction, book design, photo research, and layout services: Adventure House, NYC
Audio production: CityVox, NYC
Video production: Steadman Productions

Authors' acknowledgments

Many people contributed to the development of *Four Corners*. The authors and publisher would like to particularly thank the following **reviewers**:

Nele Noe, **Academy for Educational Development, Qatar Independent Secondary School for Girls**, Doha, Qatar; Yuan-hsun Chuang, **Soo Chow University**, Taipei, Taiwan; Celso Frade and Sonia Maria Baccari de Godoy, **Associaçao Alumni**, São Paulo, Brazil; Pablo Stucchi, **Antonio Raimondi School** and **Instituto San Ignacio de Loyola**, Lima, Peru; Kari Miller, **Binational Center**, Quito, Ecuador; Alex K. Oliveira, **Boston University**, Boston, MA, USA; Elisabeth Blom, **Casa Thomas Jefferson**, Brasilia, Brazil; Henry Grant, **CCBEU – Campinas**, Campinas, Brazil; Maria do Rosário, **CCBEU – Franca**, Franca, Brazil; Ane Cibele Palma, **CCBEU Inter Americano**, Curitiba, Brazil; Elen Flavia Penques da Costa, **Centro de Cultura Idiomas – Taubate**, Taubate, Brazil; Inara Lúcia Castillo Couto, **CEL LEP – São Paulo**, São Paulo, Brazil; Geysa de Azevedo Moreira, **Centro Cultural Brasil Estados Unidos (CCBEU Belém)**, Belém, Brazil; Sonia Patricia Cardoso, **Centro de Idiomas Universidad Manuela Beltrán**, Barrio Cedritos, Colombia; Geraldine Itiago Losada, **Centro Universitario Grupo Sol (Musali)**, Mexico City, Mexico; Nick Hilmers, **DePaul University**, Chicago, IL, USA; Monica L. Montemayor Menchaca, **EDIMSA**, Metepec, Mexico; Angela Whitby, **Edu-Idiomas Language School**, Cholula, Puebla, Mexico; Mary Segovia, **El Monte Rosemead Adult School**, Rosemead, CA, USA; Dr. Deborah Aldred, **ELS Language Centers, Middle East Region**, Abu Dhabi, United Arab Emirates; Leslie Lott, **Embassy CES**, Ft. Lauderdale, FL, USA; M. Martha Lengeling, **Escuela de Idiomas**, Guanajuato, Mexico; Pablo Frias, **Escuela de Idiomas UNAPEC**, Santo Domingo, Dominican Republic; Tracy Vanderhoek, **ESL Language Center**, Toronto, Canada; Kris Vicca and Michael McCollister, **Feng Chia University**, Taichung, Taiwan; Flávia Patricia do Nascimento Martins, **First Idiomas**, Sorocaba, Brazil; Andrea Taylor, **Florida State University in Panama**, Panamá, Panama; Carlos Lizárraga González, **Grupo Educativo Angloamericano**, Mexico City, Mexico; Dr. Martin Endley, **Hanyang University**, Seoul, Korea; Mauro Luiz Pinheiro, **IBEU Ceará**, Ceará, Brazil; Ana Lúcia da Costa Maia de Almeida, **IBEU Copacabana**, Copacabana, Brazil; Ana Lucia Almeida, Elisa Borges, **IBEU Rio**, Rio de Janeiro, Brazil; Maristela Silva, **ICBEU Manaus**, Manaus, Brazil; Magaly Mendes Lemos, **ICBEU São José dos Campos**, São José dos Campos, Brazil; Augusto Pelligrini Filho, **ICBEU São Luis**, São Luis, Brazil; Leonardo Mercado, **ICPNA**, Lima, Peru; Lucia Rangel Lugo, **Instituto Tecnológico de San Luis Potosí**, San Luis Potosí, Mexico; Maria Guadalupe Hernández Lozada, **Instituto Tecnológico de Tlalnepantla**, Tlalnepantla de Baz, Mexico; Greg Jankunis, **International Education Service**, Tokyo, Japan; Karen Stewart, **International House Veracruz**, Veracruz, Mexico; George Truscott, **Kinki University**, Osaka, Japan; Bo-Kyung Lee, **Hankuk University of Foreign Studies**, Seoul, Korea; Andy Burki, **Korea University, International Foreign Language School**, Seoul, Korea; Jinseo Noh, **Kwangwoon University**, Seoul, Korea; Nadezhda Nazarenko, **Lone Star College**, Houston, TX, USA; Carolyn Ho, **Lone Star College-Cy-Fair**, Cypress, TX, USA; Alice Ya-fen Chou, **National Taiwan University of Science and Technology**, Taipei, Taiwan; Gregory Hadley, **Niigata University of International and Information Studies, Department of Information Culture**, Niigata-shi, Japan; Raymond Dreyer, **Northern Essex Community College**, Lawrence, MA, USA; Mary Keter Terzian Megale, **One Way Línguas-Suzano**, São Paulo, Brazil; Jason Moser, **Osaka Shoin Joshi University**, Kashiba-shi, Japan; Bonnie Cheeseman, **Pasadena Community College** and **UCLA American Language Center**, Los Angeles, CA, USA; Simon Banha, **Phil Young's English School**, Curitiba, Brazil; Oh Jun Il, **Pukyong National University**, Busan, Korea; Carmen Gehrke, **Quatrum English Schools**, Porto Alegre, Brazil; Atsuko K. Yamazaki, **Shibaura Institute of Technology**, Saitama, Japan; Wen hsiang Su, **Shi Chien University, Kaohsiung Campus**, Kaohsiung, Taiwan; Richmond Stroupe, **Soka University, World Language Center**, Hachioji, Tokyo, Japan; Lynne Kim, **Sun Moon University (Institute for Language Education)**, Cheon An City, Chung Nam, Korea; Hiroko Nishikage, **Taisho University**, Tokyo, Japan; Diana Peña Munoz and Zaira Kuri, **The Anglo**, Mexico City, Mexico; Alistair Campbell, **Tokyo University of Technology**, Tokyo, Japan; Song-won Kim, **TTI (Teacher's Training Institute)**, Seoul, Korea; Nancy Alarcón, **UNAM FES Zaragoza Language Center**, Mexico City, Mexico; Laura Emilia Fierro López, **Universidad Autónoma de Baja California**, Mexicali, Mexico; María del Rocío Domíngeuz Gaona, **Universidad Autónoma de Baja California**, Tijuana, Mexico; Saul Santos Garcia, **Universidad Autónoma de Nayarit**, Nayarit, Mexico; Christian Meléndez, **Universidad Católica de El Salvador**, San Salvador, El Salvador; Irasema Mora Pablo, **Universidad de Guanajuato**, Guanajuato, Mexico; Alberto Peto, **Universidad de Oxaca**, Tehuantepec, Mexico; Carolina Rodriguez Beltan, **Universidad Manuela Beltrán, Centro Colombo Americano**, and **Universidad Jorge Tadeo Lozano**, Bogotá, Colombia; Nidia Milena Molina Rodriguez, **Universidad Manuela Beltrán** and **Universidad Militar Nueva Granada**, Bogotá, Colombia; Yolima Perez Arias, **Universidad Nacional de Colombia**, Bogota, Colombia; Héctor Vázquez García, **Universidad Nacional Autónoma de Mexico**, Mexico City, Mexico; Pilar Barrera, **Universidad Técnica de Ambato**, Ambato, Ecuador; Deborah Hulston, **University of Regina**, Regina, Canada; Rebecca J. Shelton, **Valparaiso University, Interlink Language Center**, Valparaiso, IN, USA; Tae Lee, **Yonsei University**, Seodaemun-gu, Seoul, Korea; Claudia Thereza Nascimento Mendes, **York Language Institute**, Rio de Janeiro, Brazil; Jamila Jenny Hakam, **ELT Consultant**, Muscat, Oman; Stephanie Smith, **ELT Consultant**, Austin, TX, USA.

The authors would also like to thank the Four Corners editorial, production, and new media teams, as well as the Cambridge University Press staff and advisors around the world for their contributions and tireless commitment to quality.

Scope and sequence

LEVEL 1A	Learning outcomes	Grammar	Vocabulary
Welcome Unit Pages 2–3 **Classroom language** Page 4	**Students can...** ☑ introduce themselves and others ☑ say hello and good-bye		
Unit 1 Pages 5–14			
New friends A *What's your name?* B *How do you spell it?* C *Are you a student?* D *Names and jobs*	**Students can...** ☑ ask for and say names ☑ spell names ☑ talk about where people are from and what they do ☑ discuss people's names and jobs	The verb *be* Possessive adjectives Subject pronouns *Yes / no* questions with *be*	Names and titles Interesting jobs
Unit 2 Pages 15–24			
People and places A *Where are you from?* B *What's your email address?* C *Family* D *Family and friends*	**Students can...** ☑ ask for and say people's nationalities ☑ ask for and give phone numbers and email addresses ☑ identify family members and give their ages ☑ give information about family and friends	Plural subject pronouns Questions with *be* *Who* and *How old* with *be*	Nationalities Family members Numbers 0–101
Unit 3 Pages 25–34			
What's that? A *Is this your notebook?* B *What's this called in English?* C *Clothing* D *Favorite things*	**Students can...** ☑ ask about and identify everyday items ☑ ask what something is called in English ☑ talk about clothes and possessions ☑ describe favorite possessions	Demonstratives Articles *a* and *an* Plurals Possessive pronouns *Whose* *'s* and *s'*	Everyday items Clothes and colors
Unit 4 Pages 35–44			
Daily life A *Getting around* B *What time is it?* C *My routine* D *My weekend*	**Students can...** ☑ describe how people get around ☑ ask for and tell the time ☑ ask and answer questions about routines ☑ describe the things they do on weekends	Simple present statements Simple present *yes / no* questions	Ways of getting around Days of the week and routines
Unit 5 Pages 45–54			
Free time A *Online habits* B *How much is it?* C *What do you do for fun?* D *Online fun*	**Students can...** ☑ talk about their online habits ☑ accept and decline help ☑ ask and answer questions about leisure activities ☑ discuss how they use technology	Adverbs of frequency Simple present *Wh-* questions with *do*	Online activities Leisure activities and places
Unit 6 Pages 55–64			
Work and play A *What does she do?* B *Can I speak to...?* C *Can you sing?* D *Work and study*	**Students can...** ☑ identify and talk about jobs ☑ ask for someone on the telephone ☑ have someone wait ☑ describe their talents and abilities ☑ talk about study and work programs	Simple present *Wh-* questions with *does* *Can* for ability *And*, *but*, and *or*	Jobs Abilities

Functional language	Listening and Pronunciation	Reading and Writing	Speaking
Interactions: Saying hello Saying good-bye			• Introductions • Greetings
Interactions: Asking for spelling	**Listening:** Spelling names **Pronunciation:** Contractions	**Reading:** "Famous Names" An article **Writing:** My name	• Class introductions and greetings • *Keep talking:* Name circle • Class name list • Guessing game about famous people • *Keep talking:* "Find the differences" activity about jobs and cities • Quiz about celebrities
Interactions: Asking for someone's phone number Asking for someone's email address	**Listening:** Directory Assistance calls Information forms People I know **Pronunciation:** Word stress	**Reading:** "People in My Life" Photo captions **Writing:** My friends	• True and false information about people • *Keep talking:* Interviews with new identities • Class survey for new contact information • Information exchange about family members • *Keep talking:* Family trees • Presentation about friends
Interactions: Asking what something is	**Listening:** Things around the classroom Favorite things **Pronunciation:** Plurals	**Reading:** "What's your favorite item of clothing?" A webpage **Writing:** My favorite thing	• Questions and answers about personal items • *Keep talking:* Things in the closet • Memory game about everyday items • Personal items and their owners • *Keep talking:* "Find the differences" activity about clothing colors • Presentation of favorite things
Interactions: Asking the time	**Listening:** Times of different events Angela's routine **Pronunciation:** Reduction of *to*	**Reading:** "What's your favorite day of the week?" A message board **Writing:** About my weekend	• Survey about getting to school and work • *Keep talking:* Transportation facts • Interview about the times of specific events • Interview about routines • *Keep talking:* "Find someone who" activity about routines • Survey about busy weekends
Interactions: Declining help Accepting help	**Listening:** Shopping Favorite websites **Pronunciation:** Stress in numbers	**Reading:** "Fun Online Activities" An article **Writing:** Let's chat	• Comparison of online habits • *Keep talking:* Interview about online habits • Role play of a shopping situation • Interview about leisure activities • *Keep talking:* Interviews about fun activities • Discussion about favorite websites
Interactions: Asking for someone on the phone Having someone wait	**Listening:** Telephone calls Ads for overseas programs **Pronunciation:** *Can* and *can't*	**Reading:** "Overseas Opportunities" A magazine article **Writing:** My abilities	• "Find someone who" activity about jobs • *Keep talking:* Memory game about jobs • Role play of a phone call • Interview about abilities • *Keep talking:* Board game about abilities • Discussion about study and work programs

Welcome

1 Introducing yourself

A 🔊 Listen and practice.

Simon: Hello. I'm Simon.
Chen: Hi, Simon. My name is Chen.
Nice to meet you.
Simon: Nice to meet you, too.

B Pair work Introduce yourselves.

2 Introducing someone else

A 🔊 Listen and practice.

Simon: Chen, this is my friend Sofia.
Sofia: Hi, Chen. Nice to meet you.
Chen: Nice to meet you, too, Sofia.

B Group work Introduce your partner from Exercise 1 to another classmate.

3 Hi and bye

A Listen and practice.

Simon: Hi, Chen!
Chen: Good morning, Simon! How are you?
Simon: I'm fine, thanks. And you?
Chen: Fine, thank you.

Simon: See you later, Chen!
Chen: Bye, Simon!

B Listen to the expressions. Then practice the conversation again with the new expressions.

Saying hello

Hi.

Hello.

Good morning.

Good afternoon.

Good evening.

Saying good-bye

Bye.

Good-bye.

See you.

See you later.

See you tomorrow.

C Class activity Say hello to your classmates and ask how they are.
Then say good-bye.

I can introduce myself and others. ☑
I can say hello and good-bye. ☑

Classroom language

Pair work

Group work

Class activity

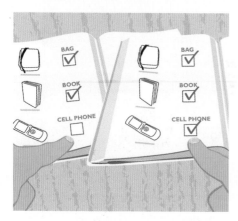

Compare answers.

Cover the picture.

Go to page 12.

What's your name?

My name is Marisa.

Ask and answer questions.

Interview your partner.

Role-play the situation.

New friends

LESSON **A**	LESSON **B**	LESSON **C**	LESSON **D**
• Names and titles • The verb *be*; possessive adjectives	• Asking for spelling	• Interesting jobs • Subject pronouns; *yes / no* questions with *be*	• Reading: "Famous Names" • Writing: My name

Warm-up

Popular names in the United States

1. Jacob
2. Michael
3. Ethan
4. Joshua
5. Daniel

1. Emma
2. Isabella
3. Emily
4. Madison
5. Ava

Source: www.ssa.gov/OACT/babynames/

A Check (✓) the popular names.

B Say ten popular names in your country.

A What's your name?

1 Language in context First day of class

🔊 Listen to Ms. Peters meet her students on the first day of class. <u>Underline</u> the names.

> Hello, everyone. I'm your teacher, <u>Ms. Peters</u>. My first name is Linda.

> Hi. What's your name?

> My name is Maria Gomez.

> Hi. I'm Maria. What are your names?

> My name is Ricardo.

> And I'm Yoko. Nice to meet you.

> What are their names?

> Her name is Yoko. His name is Ricardo.

2 Vocabulary Names and titles

A 🔊 Listen and repeat.

first name   middle name   last / family name

Jennifer Ann Wilson

full name

Miss Gomez = a single woman

Mrs. Chow = a married woman

Ms. Peters = a single or married woman

Mr. Adams = a single or married man

B Pair work Complete the sentences with your own information. Then compare answers.

My first name is _____ .

My family name is _____ .

My full name is _____ .

My teacher's name is _____ .

3 Grammar 🔊 **The verb be; possessive adjectives**

What is (What's)	your name?	**My** name **is** Maria.
	his name?	**His** name **is** Ricardo.
	her name?	**Her** name **is** Yoko.
What are	your names?	**Our** names **are** Maria and Jason.
	their names?	**Their** names **are** Ricardo and Yoko.

A Circle the correct words. Then compare with a partner.

1. Maria is a student. **His** / **Her** last name is Gomez.
2. Ms. Peters **is** / **are** our teacher. **Her** / **Their** first name is Linda.
3. My name is Jason. What's **our** / **your** name?
4. Anna and Bruce **is** / **are** students. **Her** / **Their** teacher is Miss Brown.
5. Their first names **is** / **are** Yoko and Ricardo.
6. Hello, everyone. I'm Miss Diaz. What are **your** / **his** names?

B Complete the conversation with the correct words.
Then practice in a group.

A: Hello. Welcome to English class.
What _____*is*_____ your name, please?

B: _____ name is Pam.

A: And what's _____ last name, Pam?

B: My last name _____ Nelson.

A: OK. And _____ is *your* name?

C: Ji-ah. _____ family name is Lee.

4 Speaking My name is . . .

A Class activity Meet your classmates. Say your first
and last name.

A: *Hello. My name is Oscar Martinez. What's your name?*
B: *Hi. My name is Susana Harris.*
A: *It's nice to meet you.*
B: *Nice to meet you, too.*

B Share your information.

A: *What's his name?*
B: *His name is Oscar Martinez. What's her name?*
A: *Sorry, I don't know.*

5 Keep talking!

Go to page **125** for more practice.

I can ask for and say names. ☑

B How do you spell it?

1 The alphabet

A 🔊 Listen and repeat.

A B C D E F G H I J K L M
N O P Q R S T U V W X Y Z

B **Pair work** Say a letter. Your partner points to it. Take turns.

2 Interactions   Spelling names

A 🔊 Listen and practice.

Donald: Hello. My name is Donald Wang.
Clerk: How do you spell your first name?
Donald: D-O-N-A-L-D.
Clerk: And how do you spell your last name?
Donald: W-A-N-G.

Asking for spelling

How do you spell your first name?
How do you spell your last name?

B **Pair work** Practice the conversation again with these names.

John Evans   Cindy Douglas   Antonia Lopez   Richard Wu

A: *Hello. My name is John Evans.*
B: *Hello, John. How do you spell your first name?*
A: *J-O-H-N.*
B: *And how do you spell . . . ?*

3 Listening Spell it!

A 🔊 Listen to four people spell their names. Check (✓) the correct answers.

1. ☑ Steven   2. ☐ Dina   3. ☐ Kelly   4. ☐ Bryan
    ☐ Stephen   ☐ Dena   ☐ Kerry   ☐ Brian

B 🔊 Listen to the conversations. Write the names.

1.

CITY COLLEGE
STUDENT ID

_____ Watkins

2.

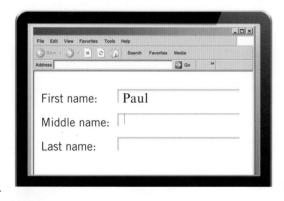

10:00 English Class

1. _____ _____

3.

24 HOUR GYM

Mr.   (Miss)   Mrs. _____

First name

Last name

4.

First name: Paul
Middle name:
Last name:

5.

Welcome, students!
Ms. _____

6.

4 Speaking A class list

Class activity Ask your classmates for their names. Make a list.

A: *What's your first name?*
B: *Tyler.*
A: *How do you spell it?*
B: *T-Y-L-E-R.*
A: *And what's your last name?*
B: *Larsen.*

First names	Last names
Tyler	Larsen
Lindsey	Fisher
Marcela	Perez
Evan	Howley
Dmitri	Benos

I can spell names. ☑

C *Are you a student?*

1 Vocabulary Interesting jobs

A 🔊 Listen and repeat.

Gael García Bernal is an **actor**. He's from Mexico.

Jeon Do-yeon is an **actress**. She's from South Korea.

Alex Hornest is an **artist**. He's from Brazil.

Brooklyn Decker is a **model**. She's from the United States.

Lang Lang is a **musician**. He's from China.

Diana Krall is a **singer**. She's from Canada.

B **Pair work** Name other people for each job.

A: *Jet Li is an actor.*
B: *Yes. And Cate Blanchett is an actress.*

2 Conversation My friend the musician

🔊 Listen and practice.

Sandy: Hey, Jacob!
Jacob: Oh, hi, Sandy. How's it going?
Sandy: Good, thanks. This is my friend Kevin.
Jacob: Hi. Nice to meet you.
Kevin: Nice to meet you, Jacob.
Jacob: Are you a student here?
Kevin: No, I'm not. I'm a musician.
Sandy: Kevin is from England.
Jacob: Oh? Are you from London?
Kevin: No, I'm not. I'm from Liverpool.

3 Grammar 🔊 Subject pronouns; *yes / no* questions with *be*

I'm a musician.	**Am I** in your class? Yes, **you are.** No, **you're not.** / No, **you aren't.**
You're a student.	**Are you** from London? Yes, **I am.** No, **I'm not.**
Kevin **is** from Liverpool. **He's** from Liverpool.	**Is he** a singer? Yes, **he is.** No, **he's not.** / No, **he isn't.**
Sandy **is** a student. **She's** a student.	**Is she** from Canada? Yes, **she is.** No, **she's not.** / No, **she isn't.**
Liverpool **is** in England. **It's** in England.	**Is your** name John? Yes, **it is.** No, **it's not.** / No, **it isn't.**

Contractions   I'm = I am   you're = you are   he's = he is   she's = she is   it's = it is

A Match the questions and the answers. Then practice with a partner.

1. Is your first name Jacob? __d__
2. Are you from Liverpool? _____
3. Is she from the United States? _____
4. Is she a musician? _____
5. Is Will Smith an actor? _____
6. Is Caracas in Peru? _____

a. No, I'm not. I'm from London.
b. Yes, he is. He's a singer, too.
c. No, she's not. She's an artist.
d. Yes, it is. And my last name is King.
e. No, it's not. It's in Venezuela.
f. Yes, she is. She's from California.

B Complete the conversations with the correct words. Then practice with a partner.

1. **A:** ____Is____ your first name Don?
   B: No, _____ not. It's Jeff.
2. **A:** _____ you from Mexico?
   B: Yes, I _____ . I'm from Mexico City.

3. **A:** _____ your teacher from England?
   B: No, she _____ .
4. **A:** _____ you a model?
   B: No, _____ not. I'm a singer.

4 Pronunciation Contractions

🔊 Listen and repeat. Notice the reduction of contractions.

I am → I'm   he is → he's   it is → it's   are not → aren't

you are → you're   she is → she's   is not → isn't

5 Speaking Ten questions

Group work Think of a famous person with a job from Exercise 1. Your group asks ten questions and guesses the name. Take turns.

A: *Is the person a man?*
B: *No, she's not.*
C: *Is she an actress?*

6 Keep talking!

Student A go to page **126** and Student B go to page **128** for more practice.

I can talk about where people are from and what they do.	☑

D **Names and jobs**

1 Reading ◀))

A Look at the pictures. What are their names?

B Read the article. Are they all singers?

★Famous Names

Actor **Tom Cruise** uses his middle name as his last name. His full name is Thomas Cruise Mapother. Tom is short for Thomas.

Zhang Ziyi is an actress from China. Zhang isn't her first name. It's her family name. In China, family names come first.

Shakira is a singer from Colombia. She uses only her first name. Her full name is Shakira Isabel Mebarak Ripoll.

Jay-Z is a hip-hop singer from the United States. Jay-Z is his nickname. His real name is Shawn Corey Carter.

Kaká is a soccer player from Brazil. His full name is Ricardo Izecson dos Santos Leite. Kaká is his nickname.

Madonna is not a nickname for this singer. It's her first name. Her full name is Madonna Louise Veronica Ciccone.

C Read the article again. Complete the sentences with the correct words.

1. Tom Cruise uses his ____*middle*____ name as his last name.
2. Shakira uses only her _____ name.
3. Ricardo Izecson dos Santos Leite's _____ is Kaká.
4. Ziyi is not Zhang Ziyi's _____ name.
5. Jay-Z's _____ name is Shawn Corey Carter.
6. Madonna Louise Veronica Ciccone is Madonna's _____ name.

D Pair work Tell your partner about another famous person's name.

"Rain is a singer, actor, and model from South Korea. Rain is his nickname.
His real name is Jeong Ji-hoon."

2 **Writing** My name

A Write sentences about your name. Use the model to help you.

> *My Name*
> *My full name is Anthony Steven Johnson. My*
> *nickname is Big Tony. Tony is short for Anthony. My*
> *middle name is Steven, and my last name is Johnson.*

B Group work Tell your group about your name.

3 **Speaking** Celebrity quiz

A Pair work Ask and answer the questions about celebrities.

1. He's an actor from Hong Kong. His initials are J. C. What's his name?

   "His name is Jackie Chan."

2. She's an actress from Spain. Her last name is Cruz. What's her first name?

3. He's a soccer player from England. His first name is David. What's his last name?

4. She's an actress and singer. Her nickname is J-Lo. What's her name?

5. He's an actor from Australia. His first name is Russell. What's his last name?

6. She's an actress from the United States. Her last name is Jolie? What's her first name?

B Pair work Create a quiz. Write three sentences about a celebrity.

> *He's a tennis player.*
> *He's from Switzerland.*
> *His first name is Roger.*

C Group work Say your sentences to another pair. They guess the celebrity. Take turns.

> **A:** *He's a tennis player.*
> **B:** *Is he Rafael Nadal?*
> **A:** *No, he isn't. He's from Switzerland.*

I can discuss people's names and jobs. ☑

Wrap-up

1 Quick pair review

Lesson A **Do you remember?** What are your classmates' last names? Answer with the information you remember. You have two minutes.

A: *Her last name is Fernandes.*
B: *Yes, it is. And his first name is Oscar. What's his last name?*
A: *It's Medina.*

Lesson B **Test your partner!** Say your full name. Can your partner write it correctly? Check his or her answer. You have two minutes.

First name	Middle name	Last / Family name

Lesson C **Brainstorm!** Make a list of interesting jobs. How many do you know? You have one minute.

Lesson D **Guess!** Describe your favorite celebrity, but don't say his or her name! Can your partner guess the name? Take turns. You have two minutes.

A: *He's a singer and a musician. He's from England. He's in Coldplay.*
B: *Is he Chris Martin?*
A: *Yes!*

2 In the real world

What is your favorite movie? Go online and find information in English about five actors or actresses in the movie. Then write about them.

• What are their names?
• Where are they from?

> *Actors in "Star Wars"*
> *My favorite movie is "Star Wars."*
> *Harrison Ford is an actor in the movie.*
> *He's from the United States . . .*

People and places

LESSON **A**
- Nationalities
- Plural subject pronouns; questions with *be*

LESSON **B**
- Asking for someone's phone number
- Asking for someone's email address

LESSON **C**
- Family members
- *Who* and *How old* with *be*

LESSON **D**
- Reading: "People in My Life"
- Writing: My friends

Warm-up

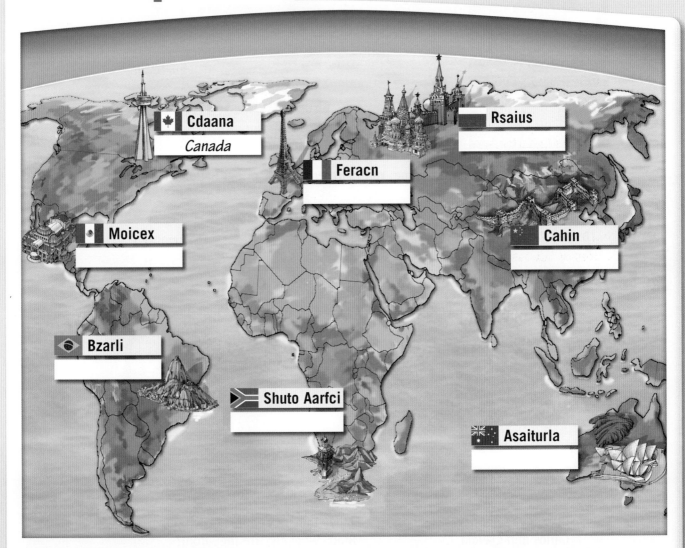

Cdaana
Canada

Rsaius

Feracn

Moicex

Cahin

Bzarli

Shuto Aarfci

Asaiturla

A Write the names of the countries.

B Say the names of five other countries in English.

A Where are you from?

1 Vocabulary Nationalities

A 🔊 Complete the chart with the correct nationalities. Then listen and check your answers.

Mexican	American	South Korean	Chilean	Greek	Colombian
Spanish	Canadian	Brazilian	Saudi	Peruvian	Japanese
British	Chinese	Turkish	Thai	Ecuadorian	✓Australian

Country		Nationality	Country		Nationality
	Australia	*Australian*		Japan	
	Brazil			Mexico	
	Britain			Peru	
	Canada			Saudi Arabia	
	Chile			South Korea	
	China			Spain	
	Colombia			Thailand	
	Ecuador			Turkey	
	Greece			the United States	

B Pair work Say a famous name. Your partner says his or her nationality. Take turns.

A: *Bill Gates.*
B: *He's from the United States. He's American.*

2 Language in context New neighbors

🔊 Listen to Brad and Emily Hill talk about their new neighbors. What are their names?

Brad: Who are they?
Emily: Oh, they're our new neighbors, Carlos and Claudia.
Brad: Are they musicians?
Emily: Yes, they are.

Brad: Where are they from?
Emily: They're from Brazil.
Brad: What city are they from?
Emily: They're from Manaus.

16

3 Grammar 🔊 | Plural subject pronouns; questions with *be*

Where are you and Sakura from?	**Where** are Carlos and Claudia from?
We're from Japan.	**They're** from Brazil.
What city are **you** from?	**What** city are **they** from?
We're from Osaka.	**They're** from Manaus.
Are you Japanese?	**Are they** Brazilian?
Yes, **we are**.	Yes, **they are**.
No, **we're not**. / No, **we aren't**.	No, **they're not**. / No, **they aren't**.

Contractions   we're = we are   they're = they are

Complete the conversations with the correct words.
Then practice with a partner.

1. **A:** Where are _____*you*_____ from?

    B: We're from Mexico.

    A: Oh? _____ city are you from? Are you from
    Mexico City?

    B: No, we _____ not. _____ from Monterrey.

2. **A:** _____ Jim and Carly American?

    B: No, they _____ . They _____ Canadian.

    A: What city in Canada are _____ from?

    B: They _____ from Toronto.

4 Pronunciation Word stress

A 🔊 Listen and repeat. Notice the stressed syllables in the nationalities.

●	●●	●●●	●●
Greek	**Brit**ish	Bra**zil**ian	Chi**nese**

B 🔊 Listen. Underline the stressed syllable in each nationality.

Japa<u>nese</u>   Australian   Spanish   Thai

5 Speaking That's not correct!

A Write three false sentences about people, countries, or nationalities.

B **Group work** Share your sentences.
Your group corrects them. Take turns.

    A: *Toronto and Vancouver are in Greece.*
    B: *No, they aren't. They're in Canada.*

> 1. *Toronto and Vancouver are in Greece.*
> 2. *Venus and Serena Williams are Ecuadorian.*
> 3. *Nicole Kidman and Russell Crowe are British.*

6 Keep talking!

Go to page **127** for more practice.

> *I can **ask for and say people's nationalities.*** ✓

1 Numbers 0 to 10; phone numbers; email addresses

A ◀)) Listen and repeat.

0 zero	1 one	2 two	3 three	4 four	5 five	6 six	7 seven	8 eight	9 nine	10 ten

B ◀)) Listen and repeat. Notice that people sometimes say "oh" for "zero" in phone numbers.

281-363-2301 = "two-eight-one, three-six-three, two-three-zero-one"

602-374-4188 = "six-oh-two, three-seven-four, four-one-eight-eight"

C ◀)) Listen and repeat. Notice the way people say email addresses.

susan8k@cup.org = "susan-eight-K-at-C-U-P-dot-org"

jun_akita@email.com = "jun-underscore-akita-at-email-dot-com"

2 Interactions   Phone numbers and email addresses

A ◀)) Listen and practice.

Stacy: Hey, Emma. What's your phone number?
Emma: It's 309-403-8708.
Stacy: What's your email address?
Emma: It's emma@cup.org.
Stacy: Thanks!

B ◀)) Listen to the expressions. Then practice the conversation again with the new expressions.

Asking for someone's phone number	*Asking for someone's email address*
What's your phone number? What's your number?	What's your email address? What's your email?

C Pair work Practice the conversation again with the information below.

978-887-8045   ej5@cup.org

604-608-4864   emma_jones@email.com

3 Listening What name, please?

A 🔊 Listen to four people call Directory Assistance for phone numbers.
Check (✓) the correct answers.

1. Carlos Moreno ☐ 333-822-1607 ☑ 323-822-1607
2. Lucy Chang ☐ 662-651-0410 ☐ 662-615-0410
3. Michael Ashcroft ☐ 866-279-9400 ☐ 866-279-9500
4. Beatriz J. Lago ☐ 341-360-7450 ☐ 341-360-4570

B 🔊 Listen to three people give their names, phone numbers, and email addresses.
Complete the forms.

MADISON ENGLISH SCHOOL

REGISTRATION

First name: _____ *Michael* _____

Middle name: _____ *John* _____

Last name: _____

Phone: _____

Email: _____

1-2-3 GYM

MEMBERSHIP

First name: _____

Middle initial: _____ *P.* _____

Last name: _____

Phone: _____

Email: _____

City Library

CARD APPLICATION

First name: _____

Family name: _____

City: _____ *Dallas* _____

Phone: _____

Email: _____

4 Speaking A new number and email address

A Write a new phone number and email address.

My new phone number: _____   My new email address: _____

B Class activity Ask five classmates for their names, new phone numbers, and
new email addresses. Complete the chart with their answers.

	Name	Phone number	Email address
1.			
2.			
3.			
4.			
5.			

C Share your information.

A: *What's her name and phone number?*
B: *Her name is Fatima. Her phone number is 212-691-3239.*
A: *What's her email address?*
B: *Her email is . . .*

| I can **ask for and give phone numbers and email addresses.** ☑ |

C Family

1 Vocabulary Family members

A 🔊 Listen and repeat.

grandmother
Sarah Mills

grandfather
Roger Mills

grandparents

mother (mom)
Helen Olson

father (dad)
Michael Olson

parents

children / kids

wife   husband

daughter   son

brother
Jack Olson

sister
Wendy Olson

brother
Brian Olson

B Pair work Ask and answer the questions about the family in Part A.

1. Are Sarah and Roger Mills single?
2. Are Michael and Helen brother and sister?
3. Are Sarah and Roger grandparents?
4. Are Wendy and Jack parents?

2 Conversation Who's that?

🔊 Listen and practice.

Lance: Who's that?
Jack: That's my sister. Her name is Wendy.
Lance: How old is she?
Jack: She's seven.
Lance: Is she your only sister?
Jack: Yeah.
Lance: And who are they?
Jack: They're my grandparents.
Lance: Wow. They look young.
And who's he?
Jack: That's me!

3 Grammar 🔊

Who and How old with be

Who's that?
   That's my sister.
How old is she?
   She's seven (years old).

Who are they?
   They're my grandparents.
How old are they?
   They're 70 and 66.

A Read the answers. Write the questions. Then practice with a partner.

A: _Who's that?_
B: Oh, that's my brother Ignacio.
A: _____
B: He's ten years old.
A: _____
B: They're my sisters Lucia, Antonia, and Carmen.
A: _____
B: They're 19, 16, and 11.
A: And _____
B: That's my grandfather.
A: _____
B: He's 62.

B Pair work Ask and answer questions about the family in Exercise 1.

A: _Who's that?_
B: _That's Jack Olson._

🔊 **Numbers 11–101**

11	eleven
12	twelve
13	thirteen
14	fourteen
15	fifteen
16	sixteen
17	seventeen
18	eighteen
19	nineteen
20	twenty
21	twenty-one
22	twenty-two
23	twenty-three
24	twenty-four
25	twenty-five
26	twenty-six
27	twenty-seven
28	twenty-eight
29	twenty-nine
30	thirty
40	forty
50	fifty
60	sixty
70	seventy
80	eighty
90	ninety
100	one hundred
101	one hundred (and) one

4 Speaking My family

A Complete the chart with information about three people in your family.

	Family member	Name	How old . . . ?	Where . . . from?
1.				
2.				
3.				

B Pair work Tell your partner about your family. Ask and answer questions for more information.

A: _Keiko is my grandmother. She's 73._
B: _Where is she from?_

5 Keep talking!

Go to page 129 for more practice.

I can **identify family members and give their ages.** ✓

D Family and friends

1 Reading 🔊

A Look at the people in Isabel's photos. Who are they? Guess.

B Read the photo descriptions. Who are Isabel's family members? Who are her friends?

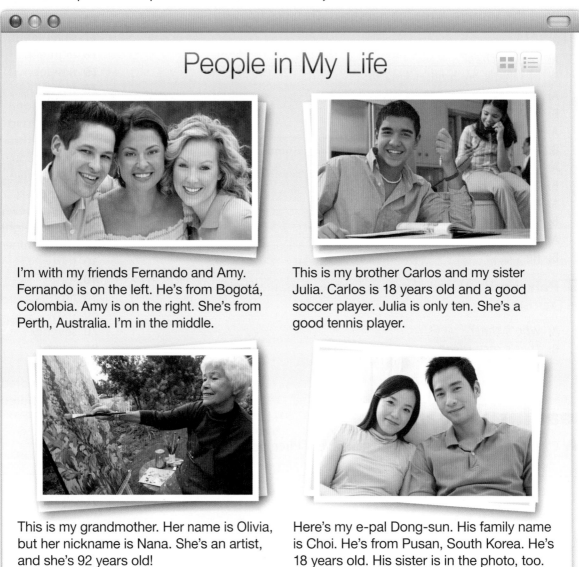

People in My Life

I'm with my friends Fernando and Amy. Fernando is on the left. He's from Bogotá, Colombia. Amy is on the right. She's from Perth, Australia. I'm in the middle.

This is my brother Carlos and my sister Julia. Carlos is 18 years old and a good soccer player. Julia is only ten. She's a good tennis player.

This is my grandmother. Her name is Olivia, but her nickname is Nana. She's an artist, and she's 92 years old!

Here's my e-pal Dong-sun. His family name is Choi. He's from Pusan, South Korea. He's 18 years old. His sister is in the photo, too.

C Read the photo descriptions again. Correct the false sentences.

1. Isabel and Amy are ~~sisters.~~   *Isabel and Amy are friends.*
2. Carlos isn't a good soccer player.   _____
3. Olivia is 90 years old.   _____
4. Isabel and Dong-sun are classmates.   _____

D Pair work Ask and answer the questions about Isabel's family and friends.

- Who are Fernando and Amy?
- What's Olivia's nickname?
- How old is Julia?
- What city is Dong-sun from?

2 Listening People I know

A 🔊 Listen to Gina show some photos to her friend. Who are the people? Check (✓) the correct answers.

1. ☐ friend
   ☑ brother

2. ☐ classmate
   ☐ sister

3. ☐ father
   ☐ grandfather

4. ☐ teacher
   ☐ mother

B 🔊 Listen again. Answer the questions.

1. How old is Mark? _____ 15 _____

2. What city is Dominique from? _____

3. What's the man's name? _____

4. Is Ms. Parker American? _____

3 Writing and speaking My friends

A Complete the chart with information about three friends. Then find photos or draw pictures of them.

	Friend 1	Friend 2	Friend 3
Name			
Age			
Nationality			
Other information			

B Write sentences about your friends in the pictures. Use the model and your answers in Part A to help you.

> **My Friends**
> My best friend is Samantha. She's 26 years old.
> She's American. She's a teacher.
> Jill is my friend, too. She's . . .

C Group work Share your pictures and sentences. Ask and answer questions for more information.

A: *This is my friend Samantha. She's 26 years old.*
B: *What's her last name?*

I can give information about family and friends. ☑

Wrap-up

1 Quick pair review

Lesson A Guess! Say five countries. Can your partner name the nationalities? Take turns. You have two minutes.

A: *South Korea.*
B: *South Korean.*

Lesson B Test your partner! Write three phone numbers and say them to your partner. Can your partner write them correctly? Check his or her answers. You have two minutes.

My phone numbers	My partner's phone numbers
_____	_____
_____	_____
_____	_____

Lesson C Brainstorm! Make a list of family words. How many do you know? You have one minute.

Lesson D Find out! Are any of your friends or family members from the same cities? You have two minutes.

A: *My father is from Mexico City, and my mother is from Guadalajara.*
B: *My grandmother is from Guadalajara, too!*

2 In the real world

Go online and find information in English about a country from another part of the world. Then write about it.

- What are five cities in the country?
- What are the names and ages of two famous people from the country?

French Cities and People
Paris, Bordeaux, Cannes, Lyon, and Dijon
are five cities in France. Marion Cotillard is
a famous actress from France. She's . . .

What's that?

LESSON A
- Everyday items
- Demonstratives; articles *a* and *an*; plurals

LESSON B
- Asking what something is

LESSON C
- Clothes and colors
- Possessive pronouns; *Whose*; *'s* and *s'*

LESSON D
- Reading: "What's your favorite item of clothing?"
- Writing: My favorite thing

Warm-up

Year: <u>*1969*</u>

Year: _____

Year: _____

Year: _____

A Label the pictures with the correct years.

✓1969   1978   1986   1994

B Can you name five things in the pictures?

A Is this your notebook?

1 Vocabulary Everyday items

A 🔊 Listen and repeat.

☐ a bag ☐ a book ☐ a cell phone ☐ a dictionary

☐ an eraser ☐ a key ☐ a laptop ☐ a notebook

☐ a pen ☐ sunglasses ☐ an umbrella ☐ a watch

B Pair work Check (✓) the things in your classroom. Then compare answers.

2 Language in context What are those?

🔊 Listen to four people talk about everyday items. Circle the items in the conversations.

Pete: Hey, Ling. What's that?
Ling: Oh, it's my dictionary.
Pete: It's nice. What are those?
Ling: They're my English books.

Susie: Are these your sunglasses?
Kyle: No, they're not.
Susie: Is this your notebook?
Kyle: Yes, it is. Thanks.

3 Grammar Demonstratives; articles *a* and *an*; plurals

What's **this**? What's **that**?

What are **these**? What are **those**?

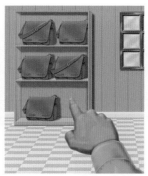

It's my dictionary.
Is **this** your dictionary?
Is **that** your dictionary?
Yes, **it is**. No, **it's not**.

They're my English books.
Are **these** your English books?
Are **those** your English books?
Yes, **they are**. No, **they're not**.

Articles a *and* an
a + consonant sound **a b**ag
an + vowel sound **an e**raser

Plurals
a book → two book**s**
a watch → two watch**es**
a dictionary → two dictionar**ies**
Note: *Sunglasses* and *glasses* are always plural.

A Complete the conversations with the correct words. Then practice with a partner.

A: What*'s this*____? A: What _____? A: What _____? A: What _____?
B: *It's a watch.*___ B: _____ B: _____ B: _____

B Pair work Ask and answer questions about everyday items in your classroom.

4 Pronunciation Plurals

Listen and repeat. Notice that some words have an extra syllable in their plural forms.

Same syllables	Extra syllables
eraser / erasers	actress / actress·es
key / keys	address / address·es
laptop / laptops	watch / watch·es

5 Speaking In my bag

Pair work Ask and answer 10 questions about the everyday items in your bags and in the classroom.

A: *Is this your English book?*
B: *No, it's not. It's my dictionary. What are those?*
A: *They're my keys.*

6 Keep talking!

Go to page 130 for more practice.

I can ask about and identify everyday items.

27

1 **Listening** Around the classroom

A 🔊 Listen to Bo and Marta ask about new words in English. Number the pictures from 1 to 5.

☐ an alarm clock ☐ a map ☐ a marker ☐ a poster 1 a remote control

B What things in Part A are in your classroom?

2 **Interactions** Asking about new words

A 🔊 Listen and practice.

Alex: Excuse me. What's this called in English?
Lucy: It's a key chain.
Alex: A key chain? How do you spell that?
Lucy: K-E-Y C-H-A-I-N.
Alex: Thanks.

B 🔊 Listen to the expressions. Then practice the conversation again with the new expressions.

Asking what something is

What's this called in English?
What's the word for this in English?
How do you say this in English?

C Pair work Practice the conversation again with the things in Exercise 1.

A: *Excuse me. What's this called in English?*
B: *It's a map.*
A: *How do you spell that?*

3 **Speaking** More everyday items

A 🔊 Listen and repeat.

1. a camera
2. a flash drive
3. a hairbrush
4. a newspaper
5. a magazine
6. a comb
7. a coin
8. a wallet

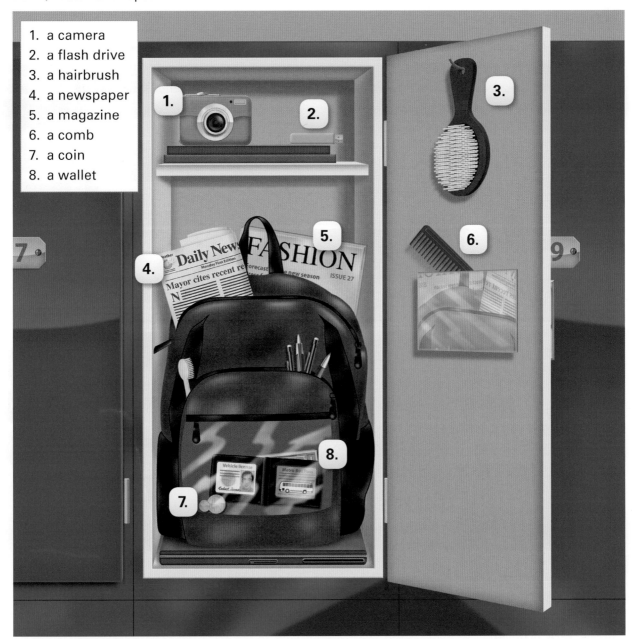

B Pair work Cover the words. What is each thing called? Answer with the information you remember.

A: *What's this called?*
B: *I think it's a . . .*

C Pair work Ask and answer questions about other things in the picture.

A: *What's the word for this in English?*
B: *It's a student I.D.*
A: *What's this called?*
B: *Hmm . . . I don't know. Let's ask the teacher.*

*I can **ask what something is called in English.*** ✓

C | Clothing

1 Vocabulary Clothes and colors

A 🔊 Listen and repeat.

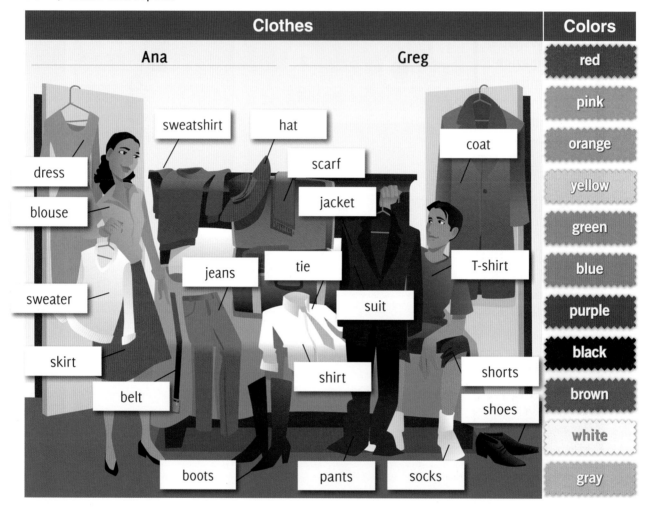

Clothes		Colors
Ana	**Greg**	red
dress	sweatshirt hat	pink
blouse	scarf	orange
	coat	yellow
	jacket	green
sweater	jeans tie T-shirt	blue
skirt	suit	purple
belt	shirt shorts	black
boots	shoes	brown
	pants socks	white
		gray

B **Pair work** Describe a classmate's clothes, but don't say his or her name!
Your partner guesses the name. Take turns.

> **A:** *His shoes are brown. His T-shirt is red and green. His pants are gray.*
> **B:** *Is it David?*

2 Conversation Whose bag is it?

🔊 Listen and practice.

Greg: Excuse me. I think that's my bag.
Laura: This bag?
Greg: Yes. I think it's mine.
Laura: It is? Oh, yes. This bag is black and yellow.
     Mine is black and green. I'm very sorry.
Greg: That's OK. Is that bag yours?
Laura: Yes, thank you.
Greg: You're welcome.

3 Grammar 🔊 | **Possessive pronouns; *Whose*; *'s* and *s'***

It's my bag. → It's **mine**.
It's your jacket. → It's **yours**.
It's his coat. → It's **his**.
They're her shoes. → They're **hers**.
They're our clothes. → They're **ours**.
It's their bag. → It's **theirs**.

Whose bag is this?
  It's Greg**'s** (bag).
Whose bag is that?
  It's the student**'s** (bag).
Whose bags are those?
  They're the student**s'** (bags).

A Circle the correct words. Then practice with a partner.

1. Whose clothes are these?
2. Are these Greg's black shoes?
3. Is this pink scarf Ana's?
4. Are these bags Greg and Ana's?
5. Whose red socks are these? Are they yours?
6. Is that my sister's skirt?

They're **your** / **our** / (**ours**).
Yes, they're **his** / **hers** / **theirs**.
No, it's not **his** / **hers** / **theirs**.
Yes, they're **his** / **hers** / **theirs**.
Yes, they're **my** / **mine** / **yours**.
No, it's not **mine** / **yours** / **hers**.

B **Pair work** Ask and answer questions about the clothing in Exercise 1.

A: *Whose jeans are these?*
B: *They're Ana's. Whose T-shirt is this?*
A: *It's . . .*

4 Speaking Yes, it's mine.

Class activity Put three of your things on a table. Then take three other things
and find their owners.

A: *Whose scarf is this?*
B: *I think it's Mary's.*
A: *Is this your scarf, Mary?*
C: *Yes, it's mine.*

5 Keep talking!

Student A go to page 131 and Student B go to page 132 for more practice.

I can talk about clothes and possessions. ✓

1 Reading)))

A Look at the pictures. What clothes and colors are they?

B Read the webpage. What countries are the people from?

What's your favorite item of clothing?
SEND US YOUR PICTURES!

This cap is my favorite. It's from my baseball team. Our team colors are blue and white.

– *Joe, the U.S.*

These boots are my favorite. I think they're from the 1970s. They're red. Red is my favorite color!

– *Ariela, Venezuela*

Here's a photo of my favorite pants. They're called *salwar*. These are men's pants, and they're from India.

– *Sadi, Canada*

This dress is my favorite item of clothing. It's called a *hanbok* in Korean. It's my mother's.

– *Bin-woo, South Korea*

Here's my favorite item of clothing. It's an old shirt. It's from London in the 1980s.

– *Ian, the U.K.*

This scarf is my favorite item of clothing. It's from Thailand. The blue color is nice.

– *Mariko, Japan*

C Read the webpage again. Answer the questions.

1. What's Joe's favorite thing? *His favorite thing is a baseball cap.*
2. What is Ariela's favorite color? _____
3. What are Sadi's pants called? _____
4. What's Bin-woo's favorite item of clothing? _____
5. Where is Ian's shirt from? _____
6. Where is Mariko's scarf from? _____

D **Pair work** What's your favorite item of clothing? Tell your partner.

"My favorite item of clothing is my blue sweatshirt."

2 Listening It's my favorite.

🔊 Listen to four people talk about their favorite things. Check (✓) the things they describe.

3 Writing and speaking My favorite thing

A Draw a picture of your favorite thing. Then answer the questions.

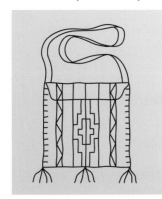

- What is it? _____
- Where is it from? _____
- How old is it? _____
- What color is it? _____

B Write about your favorite thing. Use the model and your answers in Part A to help you.

> *My Favorite Thing*
> My favorite thing is my bag. It's from Cuzco, Peru. I think it's three or four years old. It's purple, white, and yellow. I love it!

C Group work Share your drawings and your writing. Ask and answer questions for more information.

A: *Here's a picture of my favorite thing.*
B: *What is it?*
A: *It's my bag.*
C: *Where is it from?*
A: *It's from Peru.*

I can *describe my favorite possessions.* ✓

Wrap-up

1 Quick pair review

Lesson A **Brainstorm!** Make a list of everyday items and the plural forms of the words. How many do you know? You have two minutes.

Lesson B **Test your partner!** Ask your partner what the things are. You have two minutes.

Student A

Student B

Lesson C **Do you remember?** Look at your partner's clothes. Then close your eyes and describe them. Take turns. You have two minutes.

"Your shirt is green, and your jeans are blue. I think your socks are white."

Lesson D **Find out!** What is one thing both you and your partner have in your bags or desks? Find the thing and answer the questions. You have two minutes.

- What color is it?
- How old is it?
- Where is it from?

2 In the real world

What's in style? Find a picture of clothes in a magazine. Then write about them.

- What clothes are in the picture?
- What colors are the clothes?

> *Clothes in "Style Today"*
> *The woman's sweater in the picture is blue. Her pants are brown, and her shoes are black. Her bag is . . .*

Daily life

LESSON A
- Ways of getting around
- Simple present statements

LESSON B
- Asking the time

LESSON C
- Days of the week and routines
- Simple present *yes* / *no* questions

LESSON D
- Reading: "What's your favorite day of the week?"
- Writing: About my weekend

Warm-up

A Name the things you see in the picture. Use *That's a / an . . .* and *Those are . . . .*

B Say the colors of six things in the picture.

Getting around

1 Vocabulary Ways of getting around

A 🔊 Listen and repeat.

drive a car

ride a bicycle / bike

ride a motorcycle

take a taxi / cab

take the bus

take the subway

take the train

walk

B 🔊 Listen to five ways of getting around. Number them from 1 to 5.

☐ a bicycle |1| a bus   ☐ a car   ☐ a motorcycle   ☐ a train

2 Language in context Going to work and school

A 🔊 Listen to Mariela describe how she and her family get to work and school. Underline the ways they get around.

I have a car. I <u>drive</u> to work. I don't take the train.

My husband doesn't drive to work. He has a bike, so he rides his bike.

My kids walk to school. They don't take the bus.

B What about you? Check (✓) the ways you get around.

☐ I drive.   ☐ I take the bus.   ☐ I ride a bike.   ☐ I walk.

3 Grammar ◄)) Simple present statements

Regular verbs		Irregular verbs	
I **drive** to work.	I **don't take** the train.	*I / you / we / they*	*he / she / it*
You **take** a taxi.	You **don't take** the subway.	I **have** a car.	She **has** a car.
He **rides** a bike.	He **doesn't drive** to work.	You **don't have** a bike.	She **doesn't have** a bike.
She **drives**.	She **doesn't walk**.	We **go** to work.	He **goes** to work.
We **take** the train.	We **don't take** a taxi.	They **don't go** to school.	He **doesn't go** to school.
They **walk** to school.	They **don't take** the bus.		

Contractions don't = do not   doesn't = does not

A Complete the sentences with the simple present forms of the verbs. Then compare with a partner.

1. I ___take___ (take) the bus to school. I _don't walk_ (not / walk).
2. Jonathan _____ (have) a car. He _____ (drive) to work.
3. My parents _____ (take) the train to work. They _____ (go) to the city.
4. My neighbor _____ (ride) a motorcycle to work.
5. Mei-li _____ (not / take) the bus. She _____ (walk).
6. We _____ (not / have) bicycles, and we _____ (not / drive).

B Pair work Make five sentences about how your family members and friends get to school or work. Tell your partner.

A: *My sister works in a big city. She takes the bus to work.*
B: *My best friend works in a big city, too. He doesn't take the bus. He drives.*

4 Speaking I take the bus.

A Write how you get to school or work in the chart. Add extra information, such as a bus number or a train number.

	Me	Name: _____	Name: _____	Name: _____
To school				
To work				
Extra information				

B Group work Find out how three of your classmates get to school or work. Complete the chart with their information.

A: *I take the bus to school. It's the number 16 bus. How about you?*
B: *I take the bus, too. I take the number 8 bus.*

C Group work Tell another group how your classmates get to school or work.

"Daniel takes the number 8 bus to school."

5 Keep talking!

Go to page 133 for more practice.

I can describe how people get around. ✓

37

1 Telling time

A Listen and repeat.

It's twelve o'clock.

It's noon.
It's twelve p.m.

It's midnight.
It's twelve a.m.

It's twelve-oh-five.
It's five after twelve.

It's twelve-fifteen.
It's a quarter after twelve.

It's twelve-thirty.
It's half past twelve.

It's twelve-forty.
It's twenty to one.

It's twelve forty-five.
It's a quarter to one.

B Pair work Say the times in two ways.

9:45   7:30   6:03   1:15   11:40

a.m. = midnight to noon
p.m. = noon to midnight

2 Interactions   Time

A Listen and practice.

Joe: What time is it?
Mike: It's 9:15. What time is the bus?
Joe: Nine-twenty. We're early.

Keisha: What's the time?
Emily: It's 9:35. What time is our class?
Keisha: It's at 9:30. We're late!

Asking the time

What time is it?
What's the time?

B Pair work Practice the conversations again with the times below.

4:15 / 4:45   6:20 / 7:00   10:05 / 10:00   5:45 / 5:30

3 Pronunciation Reduction of *to*

A 🔊 Listen and repeat. Notice how *to* is pronounced as /tə/.

/tə/ /tə/ /tə/

It's ten to five.   It's five to two.   It's a quarter to one.

B 🔊 Listen to the conversations. Then practice them. Reduce *to* to /tə/.

A: *Is it five to one?*
B: *No, it's ten to one.*

A: *Is it ten to eight?*
B: *No, it's a quarter to eight.*

A: *Is it a quarter to three?*
B: *No, it's twenty to three.*

4 Listening Am I late?

A 🔊 Listen to five conversations about time. Write the time of each thing.

1. the movie   2. Rod's class   3. the train   4. the bus   5. Susan's class
   __10:00__   _____   _____   _____   _____

B 🔊 Listen again. Are the people early or late? Circle the correct answers.

1. (early) / late   2. early / late   3. early / late   4. early / late   5. early / late

5 Speaking What time is . . . ?

A Pair work Interview your partner. Take notes.

What time is your . . . ?

favorite class

lunch break

favorite TV show

_____   _____   _____

A: *What time is your favorite class?*
B: *It's at 7:30 a.m. What time is yours?*
A: *Mine is at 8:00 p.m. It's this class!*

B Pair work Tell another classmate about your partner's answers.

"Ji-sung's favorite class is at 7:30 a.m."

I can *ask for and tell the time.* ☑

39

C My routine

1 Vocabulary Days of the week and routines

A ◄)) Listen and repeat.

Weekdays					The weekend	
Monday	Tuesday	Wednesday	Thursday	Friday	Saturday	Sunday

B ◄)) Listen and repeat.

get up   drink coffee   eat breakfast   read the news   go to school

exercise   cook dinner   study   watch TV   go to bed

C Pair work What is your routine on weekdays? on weekends? Tell your partner.

"I get up and eat breakfast on weekdays. I go to school. I study . . ."

2 Conversation Monday morning

◄)) Listen and practice.

Tom: It's Monday morning . . . again!
 Liz: Do you get up early on weekdays?
Tom: Yes, I do. I get up at 5:30 a.m.
 Liz: Wow! That *is* early!
Tom: And I study all morning and afternoon.
 Liz: Do you study in the evenings, too?
Tom: No, I don't. I cook dinner, exercise, and go to bed late, after midnight.
 Liz: That's not good. What about on weekends?
Tom: On weekends, I sleep!

3 Grammar

Simple present *yes* / *no* questions

Do you **go** to school on Mondays?
   Yes, I **do.**   No, I **don't.**

Does Liz **exercise**?
   Yes, she **does.**   No, she **doesn't.**

Do you and your friends **watch** TV?
   Yes, we **do.**   No, we **don't.**

Do your friends **study**?
   Yes, they **do.**   No, they **don't.**

A Write *yes* / *no* questions with the information below. Then compare with a partner.

1. (you / get up / 7:00)   *Do you get up at 7:00?*
2. (you / read the news / every day)
3. (your teacher / drink coffee / in class)
4. (your parents / watch TV / in the evening)
5. (your friend / exercise / on weekends)
6. (you and your friends / study / after midnight)

B Pair work Ask and answer the questions in Part A. Answer with your own information.

> **A:** *Do you get up at 7:00?*
> **B:** *No, I don't. I get up at 6:00 on weekdays and 9:30 on weekends.*

4 Speaking Routines

A Pair work Interview your partner. Check (✓) his or her answers.

Do you . . . ?	Yes	No
cook dinner on weekends	☐	☐
drink coffee after 7:00 p.m.	☐	☐
exercise every day	☐	☐
go to bed late on weekdays	☐	☐
get up early on weekdays	☐	☐
read the news in the evening	☐	☐

> **A:** *Do you cook dinner on weekends?*
> **B:** *No, I don't. I cook on weekdays!*

B Pair work Tell another classmate about your partner's routines.

> **A:** *Does Rita cook dinner on weekends?*
> **B:** *No, she doesn't. She cooks on weekdays!*

Time expressions

on Sunday(s)
on Sunday afternoon(s)
on weekdays
on the weekend
on weekends
in the morning(s)
in the afternoon(s)
in the evening(s)
at noon / midnight
at night
before 7:00
after midnight
every day

5 Keep talking!

Go to page **134** for more practice.

I can ask and answer questions about routines. ☑

D My weekend

1 Reading 🔊

A Look at the message board question. What's *your* favorite day of the week? Why?

B Read the message board. Whose favorite day is on the weekend?

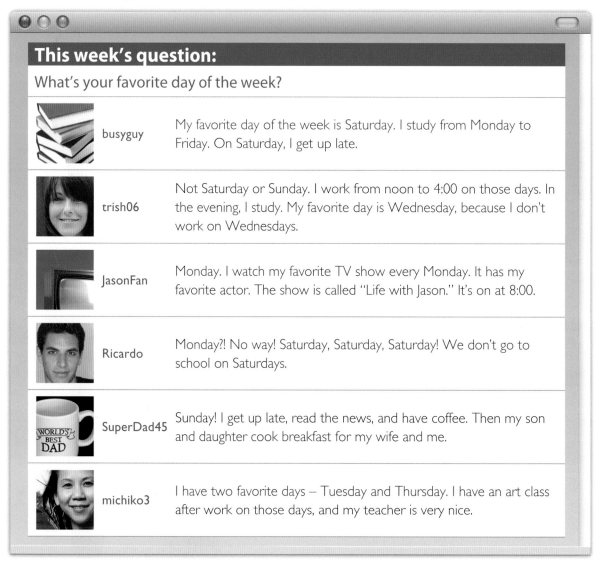

This week's question:

What's your favorite day of the week?

	busyguy	My favorite day of the week is Saturday. I study from Monday to Friday. On Saturday, I get up late.
	trish06	Not Saturday or Sunday. I work from noon to 4:00 on those days. In the evening, I study. My favorite day is Wednesday, because I don't work on Wednesdays.
	JasonFan	Monday. I watch my favorite TV show every Monday. It has my favorite actor. The show is called "Life with Jason." It's on at 8:00.
	Ricardo	Monday?! No way! Saturday, Saturday, Saturday! We don't go to school on Saturdays.
	SuperDad45	Sunday! I get up late, read the news, and have coffee. Then my son and daughter cook breakfast for my wife and me.
	michiko3	I have two favorite days – Tuesday and Thursday. I have an art class after work on those days, and my teacher is very nice.

C Read the message board again. What's each person's favorite day? Why?
Complete the chart.

	Favorite day(s)	**Why?**
1. busyguy	*Saturday*	*gets up late*
2. trish06	_____	_____
3. JasonFan	_____	_____
4. Ricardo	_____	_____
5. SuperDad45	_____	_____
6. michiko3	_____	_____

D Class activity What's your class's favorite day? Vote and discuss your answer.

2 **Listening** Angela's routine

A 🔊 Listen to Angela talk about her routine on weekends. Circle the activities she does.

Saturdays		Sundays	
(work)	watch TV	get up late	exercise
go to class	go to bed late	study	cook

B 🔊 Listen again. Write one more thing Angela does on Saturdays and on Sundays.

On Saturdays: _____   On Sundays: _____

3 **Writing** About my weekend

A Complete the chart with information about your weekend routine. Include two activities you do and two activities you don't do.

Saturdays	Sundays
Activities I do:	Activities I do:
• _____	• _____
• _____	• _____
Activities I don't do:	Activities I don't do:
• _____	• _____
• _____	• _____

B Write about your weekend routine. Use the model and your answers in Part A to help you.

C **Group work** Share your writing. Ask and answer questions for more information.

> *My Weekend Routine*
> *On Saturdays, I get up late and watch TV. I don't study, and I don't go to work. On Sundays, . . .*

4 **Speaking** Are you busy?

A Add two questions about routines to the survey. Then circle your answers.

ARE YOU BUSY?	Me		You	
1. Do you study English every weekend?	Yes	No	Yes	No
2. Do you go to work on the weekend?	Yes	No	Yes	No
3. Do you get up before 7:00 on the weekend?	Yes	No	Yes	No
4. Do you exercise on the weekend?	Yes	No	Yes	No
5.	Yes	No	Yes	No
6.	Yes	No	Yes	No

B **Pair work** Interview your partner. Circle his or her answers. Is your partner busy?

I can describe the things I do on weekends. ☑

Wrap-up

1 Quick pair review

Lesson A **Brainstorm!** Make a list of ways of getting around. How many do you know? You have one minute.

Lesson B **Test your partner!** Say four different times. Can your partner write them correctly? Check his or her answers. You have two minutes.

Lesson C **Guess!** Say a time and a day. Can your partner guess your routine at that time? Take turns. You have two minutes.

A: *Two o'clock on Monday.*
B: *Do you exercise at 2:00 on Monday?*
A: *No.*
B: *Do you study?*
A: *Yes.*

Lesson D **Find out!** What are three things both you and your partner do on weekends? You have two minutes.

A: *I exercise on Saturday mornings. How about you?*
B: *No, I don't. I go to bed late on Saturdays. How about you?*
A: *Yes, I do!*

2 In the real world

What time is it around the world? Go online and find the local time in these cities.

Beijing	Cairo	Los Angeles	Rio de Janeiro	Tokyo
Buenos Aires	London	Mexico City	Sydney	Toronto

What time is it now?
It is nine o'clock in the evening in Beijing now. In Buenos Aires, it's . . .

Free time

LESSON A	LESSON B	LESSON C	LESSON D
• Online activities • Adverbs of frequency	• Declining help • Accepting help	• Leisure activities and places • Simple present *Wh-* questions with *do*	• Reading: An article • Writing: An online chat

Warm-up

A Look at the pictures. Make two sentences about each one.

B When do you have free time? Write the times.

	Monday	Tuesday	Wednesday	Thursday	Friday	Saturday	Sunday
a.m.							
p.m.							

A *Online habits*

1 **Vocabulary** Online activities

A 🔊 Listen and repeat.

☐ chat with friends

☐ check email

☐ download music

☐ play games

☐ post comments

☐ search the Internet

☐ shop online

☐ upload videos

B Pair work Check (✓) the things you do online. Then tell your partner.

"I download music, post comments, and play games. How about you?"

2 **Language in context** Habits survey

A 🔊 Read the survey about online habits. Circle the online activities.

Habits survey

1. Do you ever shop online?
   ☑ Yes, I often shop online.
   ☐ Yes, I sometimes shop online.
   ☐ No, I never shop online.

2. Do you ever download music?
   ☐ Yes, I often download music.
   ☑ Yes, I sometimes download music.
   ☐ No, I never download music.

3. Do you ever post comments on blogs?
   ☐ Yes, I often post comments.
   ☐ Yes, I sometimes post comments.
   ☑ No, I never post comments.

B What about you? Do you do the online activities in the survey?

3 Grammar 🔊 Adverbs of frequency

	always		100%	Do you **ever** shop online?
	usually			
	often			Yes, I sometimes shop online. /
I	sometimes	shop online.		Yes, I sometimes do.
	hardly ever			No, I never shop online. /
	never		0%	No, I never do.

A Rewrite the conversations with the adverbs of frequency. Then practice with a partner.

1. **A:** Do you download movies? (ever)   *Do you ever download movies?*

   B: Yes, I download movies. (often)   _____

2. **A:** Do you check email in class? (ever)   _____

   B: No, I check email in class. (never)   _____

3. **A:** Do you play games online? (ever)   _____

   B: Yes, I do. (usually)   _____

4. **A:** Do you post comments online? (ever)   _____

   B: No, I do that. (hardly ever)   _____

B Pair work Ask and answer the questions in Part A. Answer with your own information.

A: *Do you ever download movies?*
B: *Yes, I sometimes do.*

4 Speaking Often, sometimes, or never?

A Complete the chart with information about your online habits. Use the ideas in Exercise 1 and your own ideas.

I often . . .	I sometimes . . .	I never . . .
•	•	•
•	•	•

B Group work Compare your online habits.

A: *I often play games online.*
B: *Oh? I never do that.*
C: *I sometimes do.*

5 Keep talking!

Go to page 135 for more practice.

I can talk about my online habits. ✓

47

1 Prices

A 🔊 Listen and repeat.

$79.00	=	seventy-nine dollars
$79.95	=	seventy-nine dollars and ninety-five cents
	OR	seventy-nine ninety-five
$379.95	=	three hundred seventy-nine dollars and ninety-five cents
	OR	three seventy-nine ninety-five

B 🔊 Listen and practice.

A: *How much is this?* **A:** *How much are these?* **A:** *How much is that watch?*
B: *It's $54.89.* **B:** *They're $234.99.* **B:** *It's only $109.25.*

C Pair work Practice the conversations again. Say the prices in a different way.

2 Interactions **At the store**

A 🔊 Listen and practice.

Salesperson: Hello.
Margaret: Hi.
Salesperson: Can I help you?
Margaret: No, thanks. I'm just looking.

Salesperson: Can I help you?
Renato: Yes, please. How much is this camera?
Salesperson: It's $169.50.
Renato: Thanks.

B 🔊 Listen to the expressions. Then practice the conversations again with the new expressions.

Declining help	**Accepting help**
No, thanks. I'm just looking.	Yes, please.
No. I'm fine, thanks.	Yes, thanks.

3 Pronunciation Thirteen or thirty?

A 🔊 Listen and repeat. Notice the difference in stress in the numbers.

B 🔊 Listen to four conversations about prices. Circle the correct prices.

1. (\$14) / \$40   3. \$17 / \$70
2. \$16 / \$60   4. \$19 / \$90

C Pair work Say a number from the chart. Your partner points to it. Take turns.

Last syllable	First syllable
13 thir**teen**	30 **thir**ty
14 four**teen**	40 **for**ty
15 fif**teen**	50 **fif**ty
16 six**teen**	60 **six**ty
17 seven**teen**	70 **se**venty
18 eigh**teen**	80 **eigh**ty
19 nine**teen**	90 **nine**ty

4 Listening Can I help you?

A 🔊 Listen to four conversations in a store. Check (✓) the words you hear.

1. ✓ camera   2. ☐ shirts   3. ☐ bag   4. ☐ scarf
   ☐ cell phone   ☐ skirt   ☐ bags   ☐ shorts
   ☐ laptop   ☐ T-shirt   ☐ belt   ☐ skirt

B 🔊 Listen to a salesperson offer help to four customers. Do the customers accept or decline help? Circle the correct answers.

1. (accept) / decline   2. accept / decline   3. accept / decline   4. accept / decline

5 Speaking Role play

Class activity Role-play the situation. Then change roles.

Group A: You are salespeople. Offer help to the customers. Answer questions about prices.

Group B: You are customers. Decline help three times. Then accept help three times, and ask for the prices of three items.

$168.95

$23.99

$877.50

$40.89

$219.00

$9.25

A: *Can I help you?*
B: *No, thanks. I'm just looking.*

OR

A: *Can I help you?*
B: *Yes, please. How much . . . ?*

> I can *accept and decline help.* ☑

C *What do you do for fun?*

1 **Vocabulary** Leisure activities and places

A 🔊) Listen and repeat.

eat out

go dancing

go shopping

hang out

play soccer

watch movies

B 🔊) Listen and repeat.

at a club

at a restaurant

at home

at the mall

in / at the park

C Pair work Do you do the activities in Part A? Where? Tell your partner.

A: *I watch movies at home. Do you?*
B: *Yes, I do. I watch movies at the mall, too.*

2 **Conversation** In our free time

🔊) Listen and practice.

Annie: What do you do for fun, Chad?
Chad: Oh, I hang out with friends.
Annie: Yeah? Where do you hang out?
Chad: At the mall. We sometimes watch a movie
or go shopping. What about you?
Annie: I play soccer in the park.
Chad: Sounds fun. Who do you play with?
Annie: My brother and his friends. Actually, we
need another player. Are you interested?
Chad: Yeah!

3 Grammar 🔊 | Simple present *Wh-* questions with *do*

What do you do for fun?	**Who do** you play soccer with?
I hang out.	My brother and his friends.
Where do you hang out?	**When do** you usually play soccer?
At the mall.	We usually play on weekends.
How do you get there?	**Why do** you play soccer?
We take the bus.	Because it's my favorite sport.

A Read the answers. Write *Wh-* questions. Then practice with a partner.

1. *How do you get to class?*   I take the bus to class.
2. _____ I eat out on Friday night.
3. _____ I play sports with my brother.
4. _____ I go shopping at the mall.
5. _____ My friends and I watch movies on Saturday.
6. _____ I sometimes study with my friends.

B Pair work Ask and answer the questions in Part A. Answer with your own information.

A: *How do you get to class?*
B: *I usually walk, but I sometimes take the subway.*

4 Speaking Tell me more!

A Pair work Interview your partner. Take notes.

Questions	Name: _____
1. When do you usually check your email?	
2. What time do you go to bed on Sundays?	
3. When do you chat with friends?	
4. Who do you eat out with? Where do you go?	
5. Where do you go shopping? How do you get there?	
6. What do you do for fun on weekends? Why?	

B Pair work Tell another classmate about your partner's answers. Are any of your partners' answers the same?

A: *Celia usually checks her email at night.*
B: *Luis checks his email at night, too.*

5 Keep talking!

Go to page **136** for more practice.

I can *ask and answer questions about leisure activities.* ☑

51

Online fun

1 Reading 🔊

A Look at the pictures in the article. What do you see?

B Read the article. What's the best title? Check (✓) the correct answer.

☐ New Websites   ☐ Chat Online   ☐ Fun Online Activities

Try one of these activities in your free time.

1 *Buy and Sell*
What do you want? A new video game? A new phone? What *don't* you want? Your old jeans? Your old schoolbooks? Buy and sell things online!

2 _____
Where is your best friend from elementary school now? Does your friend live in your city? Search his or her name, and find your friend.

3 _____
Do you have pictures or movies on your cell phone or camera? Post them! Upload your favorite photos and videos for friends.

4 _____
Tour a museum from your home! Go to the Egyptian Museum in Cairo, Barcelona's Picasso Museum, or Kyoto's National Museum.

5 _____
Where do you want to go? Search the address and city, and find a map. Get directions to stores, parks, or a new restaurant.

6 _____
Do you want a new album, your favorite song, or a new ringtone for your cell phone? Download it.

C Read the article again. Where do the headings go? Write them in the article.

Map it!	Take a Tour	Share Photos and Videos
Get Music	✓Buy and Sell	Find an Old Friend

D Pair work What activities do you do online? Tell your partner.

"I hardly ever sell things online, but I sometimes buy clothes online."

2 Listening Four websites

A 🔊 Listen to Allison and James talk about the pictures on four websites.
Number the pictures from 1 to 4.

B 🔊 Listen again. Correct the false sentences.

photos
1. Allison looks at ~~videos~~ of Lorena Ochoa.   3. James buys clothes on the website.

2. The Museum of Modern Art is in Paris.   4. James often uploads videos.

3 Writing Let's chat!

A Choose a topic for a "chat": free time, online activities, or school. Create a user name. Then write a question about your topic.

B Group work Pass your question to the classmate on your right. Read and answer your classmate's question. Continue to pass, read, and answer all of the questions in your group.

> *techgirl:* What do you do in your free time?
>
> *jae-min:* I watch TV and play video games. My favorite video game is Soccer Star.
>
> *jramirez:* I hardly ever play video games. I usually watch TV at night. My favorite show is . . .

C Class activity Tell the class about your chat.

4 Speaking My favorite website

A Group work Add a question about online habits to the list. Then ask and answer the questions.

- What's your favorite website?
- What other websites do you usually go to?
- Where do you upload your photos and videos?
- What news websites do you read?
- What blogs do you read?
- _____

B Class activity Share your information. Which websites are popular?

I can discuss how I use technology. ☑

Wrap-up

1 Quick pair review

Lesson A **Brainstorm!** Make a list of online activities. How many do you know? You have one minute.

Lesson B **Test your partner!** Write three prices and say them to your partner. Can your partner write them correctly? Check his or her answers. You have two minutes.

My prices	My partner's prices
_____	_____
_____	_____
_____	_____

Lesson C **Find out!** What are three activities both you and your partner do for fun? You have two minutes.

A: *I play soccer for fun. Do you?*
B: *No, I don't play soccer. Do you go shopping for fun?*
A: *Yes, sometimes.*

Lesson D **Do you remember?** Complete the sentences with the correct words. You have one minute.

✓Buy   Find   Share   Take

1. ____*Buy*____ and sell online.   3. _____ an old friend.
2. _____ photos and videos.   4. _____ a tour.

2 In the real world

How much are they? Find two different prices for each of these items. Then write about them.

a belt	jeans	a small camera
a downloaded song	a laptop	an umbrella

> *Different Prices*
> A black belt is $29.99 at Style Shop.
> It's $20.00 at Kelly's Accessories.
> A downloaded song is . . .

Work and play

LESSON A
- Jobs
- Simple present *Wh-* questions with *does*

LESSON B
- Asking for someone on the phone
- Having someone wait

LESSON C
- Abilities
- *Can* for ability; *and*, *but*, and *or*

LESSON D
- Reading: "Overseas Opportunities"
- Writing: My abilities

Warm-up

A Where do the people usually work? Match the people and the places.

B Do you know any of the jobs in the pictures? Do you know any other jobs?

A What does she do?

1 Vocabulary Jobs

A 🔊 Match the jobs and the people. Then listen and check your answers.

a. accountant	c. doctor	e. flight attendant	g. pilot	i. receptionist	✓k. waiter
b. cook / chef	d. electrician	f. nurse	h. police officer	j. taxi driver	l. waitress

B Pair work Point to people in the pictures, and ask what their jobs are. Your partner says the jobs. Take turns.

> **A:** *What's his job?*
> **B:** *He's a waiter.*

2 Language in context At work

A 🔊 Read two job profiles. What are their jobs?

Lucia Ortega works in a hospital
from 11:00 p.m. to 7:00 a.m.
What does Lucia do? She's a nurse.

Henry Jenkins works in an office. He's an
accountant. What company does Henry work for?
He works for A1 Accountants.

B What about you? Do you have a job? What is it?

3 Grammar 🔊   **Simple present *Wh-* questions with *does***

What does Lucia **do**?	**Where does** Henry **work**?
She's a nurse.	He works in an office.
When does she **work**?	**What** company **does** Henry **work** for?
She works from 11:00 to 7:00.	He works for A1 Accountants.

A Complete the conversations with the correct words. Then practice with a partner.

1. **A:** ___What___ does your brother ___do___ ?
   B: Oh, Tom's a doctor.
   A: Really? _____ does he _____ ?
   B: He works in a hospital.

2. **A:** _____ does Sue _____ ?
   B: On Mondays, Wednesdays, and Fridays.
   A: And _____ company does she _____ for?
   B: She works for Town Bank.

B Pair work Write questions about Mr. Miller, Lisa, and Nicole.
Then ask and answer them.

What _does Mr. Miller do_____ ? What _____ ? Where _____ ?
Where _____ ? When _____ ? What company _____ ?

A: *What does Mr. Miller do?*
B: *He's an English teacher.*

4 Speaking   People's jobs

Class activity Add two jobs to the chart. Then find classmates who know people
with those jobs. Ask for more information.

Job	Classmate	Person	Extra information
chef			
nurse			
police officer			
taxi driver			

A: *Do you know a chef?*   **A:** *Where does he work?*
B: *Yes. My friend Marco is a chef.*   **B:** *He works at Speedy Sushi.*

5 Keep talking!

Go to page 137 for more practice.

Go to page 137 for more practice.

> *I can identify and talk about jobs.* ☑

B Can I speak to . . . ?

1 Interactions · On the phone

A Look at the pictures. Where does Ed work?

B 🔊 Listen and practice.

> **Ed:** Good morning, Ace Accountants.
> **Ashley:** Hello. Can I speak to Laura Reed?
> **Ed:** Who is this, please?
> **Ashley:** It's Ashley Tillman.

> **Ed:** Just a minute, please. . . . Oh, I'm
> sorry. Ms. Reed is in a meeting.
> **Ashley:** All right. Thank you.

C 🔊 Listen to the expressions. Then practice the conversation again with the new expressions.

Asking for someone on the phone
Can I speak to . . . ? Could I please speak to . . . ? Is . . . there?

Having someone wait
Just a minute, please. Hold on, please. One moment, please.

D Pair work Practice the conversation again with the names below.

Gabriela Garcia   Anthony Davis   Kumiko Takahashi   Roberto Santos

A: *Good morning, Ace Accountants.*
B: *Hello. Can I speak to Gabriela Garcia?*
A: *Who is this, please?*

2 Listening A busy woman

A 🔊 Listen to Kevin call Star Computers on five different days. Where is Ellen Astor each day? Number the pictures from 1 to 5.

at lunch

in a meeting

on another line

on vacation

with a customer

B 🔊 Listen again. How does Kevin ask to speak to Ellen Astor? Number the questions from 1 to 5.

_____ Is Ms. Astor there?

_____ Could I please speak to . . . ?

_1_ Can I please speak to Ellen Astor?

_____ Can I speak to Ellen Astor?

_____ Could I speak to Ms. Astor, please?

3 Speaking Role play

Pair work Role-play the situation. Then change roles.

Student A: You are a receptionist at Sun Travel. Answer the phone. Tell the caller to wait, and then say why the person can't talk.

Student B: Call Sun Travel. Imagine someone you know works there. Ask to speak to the person.

A: *Hello, Sun Travel.*
B: *Hi. Can I please speak to Jackie Miller?*
A: *Of course. Just a minute, please. . . .*
I'm sorry. Jackie's with a customer.
B: *Oh, OK. Thanks.*

> *I can **ask for someone on the telephone**.* ☑
> *I can **have someone wait**.* ☑

C Can you sing?

1 Vocabulary Abilities

A 🔊 Listen and repeat.

dance

draw

fix computers

paint

play the guitar

sing

speak French

Où est la piscine?

swim

B Pair work What things do you sometimes do? Tell your partner.

2 Conversation Top talent?

🔊 Listen and practice.

Host: Welcome to *Top Talent*. What's your name, please?

Pamela: Hello. My name is Pamela Wells.

Host: Tell us, can you sing, Pamela?

Pamela: No, I can't sing at all.

Host: Well, can you play an instrument? the guitar? the piano?

Pamela: No, I can't.

Host: You can't sing, and you can't play an instrument. What *can* you do, Pamela?

Pamela: I can dance!

Host: Great! Let's see.

3 Grammar · **Can for ability; *and*, *but*, and *or***

I	
You	
He	**can** dance very well.
She	**can't** sing at all.
We	
They	

Can you sing?
    Yes, I **can**.   No, I **can't**.
What **can** Pamela do?
    She **can** dance, **and** she **can** swim.
    She **can** dance, **but** she **can't** sing.
    She **can't** sing **or** play an instrument.

A Read the answers. Write the questions. Then practice with a partner.

1. *Can Jenny swim?*   No, Jenny can't swim.
2. _____   Billy can fix computers.
3. _____   Yes, Tom and Jill can sing very well.
4. _____   No, I can't play an instrument.
5. _____   Jay and I can dance and speak French.
6. _____   No, Sally can't paint at all.

B Pair work Make six sentences about Frank with *and*, *but*, or *or*. Tell your partner.

Frank's Abilities
✓ draw   X sing   ✓ swim
X paint   X dance   ✓ play the guitar

"Frank can draw, but . . ."

4 Pronunciation *Can* and *can't*

A Listen and repeat. Notice the pronunciation of *can* /kən/ and *can't* /kænt/.

I can draw.   I can't paint.   I can draw, but I can't paint.

B Listen to the conversations. Do you hear *can* or *can't*? Circle the correct answers.

1. can /(can't)   2. can / can't   3. can / can't   4. can / can't

5 Speaking Can you paint?

A Pair work Add two abilities to the chart. Then interview your partner. Check (✓) the things he or she can do.

Can you . . . ?			
☐ paint	☐ upload a video	☐ sing in English	☐ ride a bicycle
☐ draw	☐ dance	☐ play an instrument	☐
☐ swim	☐ drive	☐ fix a car	☐

B Pair work Tell another classmate about your partner's abilities. Can your partner do something that you can't? What is it?

6 Keep talking!
Go to page 138 for more practice.

I can *describe my talents and abilities.* ✓

61

1 Reading 🔊

A Look at the pictures. Where do they work? Guess.

B Read the article. Where are Jin-hee, Ramiro, and Aisha now?

OVERSEAS OPPORTUNITIES
FOR STUDENTS

Be an Intern

You work for a short time in a company or an organization. You sometimes get a small salary as an intern.

Jin-hee is from South Korea and has an internship with a publishing company in New York City. The company makes French books. Jin-hee answers the phone and makes photocopies.

Study and Work

In this program, you can study *and* work. You usually study in the morning and work in the afternoon or evening.

Ramiro is from Mexico. He's in Australia now. He studies computer science part-time and works part-time. He takes classes in the morning and fixes computers in the evening. He works 20 hours a week.

Volunteer

Some organizations need extra help. Volunteers usually don't get a salary for their work.

Aisha is from Egypt. She's on a volunteer program in Nigeria at a school for children. She teaches classes, and she helps the children with their schoolwork. She works full-time from Monday to Friday.

C Read the article again. Answer the questions.

1. Do people get a salary as an intern? _*They sometimes get a small salary.*_
2. What does Jin-hee do as an intern? _____
3. In study and work programs, when do people usually work? _____
4. What does Ramiro study? _____
5. Do volunteers usually get a salary for their work? _____
6. What does Aisha do as a volunteer? _____

D Pair work Do people come to your country from other countries to study or work? What do they do? Discuss your ideas.

2 Listening Exciting opportunities

A 🔊 Listen to two students discuss three advertisements. Number them from 1 to 3.

Volunteer!

Are you interested in animals? Can you swim? _____ with turtles in Costa Rica. Work _____ to Saturday, 6:00 a.m. to _____ p.m. For more information, send an email to **CRVolunteer@cup.edu**

Be an Intern

Are you 18 to _____ years old? Can you speak Chinese, _____ , Japanese, or English? Be an intern at a theme _____ in Hong Kong!

Email us at **hongkong@cup.com/intern**

Study and Work

Can you cook? Come to Rome. Study Italian in the morning, and work in a restaurant in the _evening_ . See the city in your _____ time! _____ salary. Contact us at **study&work@cambridge.org**

1

B 🔊 Listen again. Complete the sentences with the correct words.

3 Writing My abilities

A Make lists of things you can and can't do well. Then write a paragraph about your abilities. Use the model and your lists to help you.

> *My Abilities*
> *I can play sports. I can play basketball and tennis very well. My favorite sport is soccer, but I can't play it very well. I can't play golf at all!*

B Pair work Share your paragraphs. Ask and answer questions for more information.

4 Speaking How well can you . . . ?

Group work Discuss the overseas opportunities in Exercise 1, Exercise 2, or your own ideas.

- What abilities do you need in each program?
- How well can you do each thing? (very well? well? not well? not at all?)
- Are any of the programs right for you?

I can *talk about study and work programs.* ✓

Wrap-up

1 Quick pair review

Lesson A **Guess!** Describe a job, but don't say what it is. Can your partner guess it? Take turns. You have two minutes.

A: *This person drives a car.*
B: *Is he a police officer?*
A: *No. The car is yellow in New York City.*
B: *Is he a taxi driver?*
A: *Yes.*

Lesson B **Brainstorm!** Make a list of ways to ask for someone on the phone and have someone wait. You have two minutes.

Lesson C **Find out!** What are two things both you and your partner can do? What are two things you can't do? You have two minutes.

A: *Can you cook?*
B: *Not really. Can you?*
A: *No, I can't!*

Lesson D **Do you remember?** Are the sentences true or false? Write T (true) or F (false). You have two minutes.

1. Volunteers usually get a salary. _F_

2. Volunteers always work part-time. _____

3. Interns work for companies or organizations. _____

4. Interns never get a salary. _____

2 In the real world

Go online and find information in English about an overseas program.
Then write about it.

- What is the name of the program?
- Where is the program?
- What kind of program is it?
- What do people do in the program?

> *The Peace Corps*
> *The Peace Corps is an overseas program.*
> *Americans volunteer in many countries.*
> *They help build things and teach people.*

Name circle

A **Group work** Stand in a circle. Go around the circle and say your first names.
Repeat your classmates' names before you say your own name.

B **Group work** Go around the circle again. Repeat your classmates' full names.

A: *My name is Eduardo Sanchez.*
B: *His name is Eduardo Sanchez. My name is Ming-mei Lee.*
C: *His name is Eduardo Sanchez. Her name is Ming-mei Lee. My name . . .*

Entertainment awards

Student A

Pair work You and your partner have pictures of the same people, but some of the jobs and cities are different. Ask questions to find the differences. Circle them.

A: *Is Antonio Loren a model in your picture?*
B: *Yes, he is.*
A: *OK. That's the same. Is he from Rome?*
B: *No, he's from Milan. That's different.*

Around the world

A Create a "new" identity. Write your new name and the country and city you are from.

Name:

Country:

City:

B **Group work** Interview four classmates. Complete the cards with their "new" identities.

Name:

Country:

City:

Name:

Country:

City:

Name:

Country:

City:

Name:

Country:

City:

A: *Hi. What's your name?*

B: *Hi. My name is Sophie Manet.*

A: *Where are you from, Sophie?*

B: *I'm from France.*

A: *Oh, you're French. What city are you from?*

B: *I'm from Paris.*

Entertainment awards

Student B

Pair work You and your partner have pictures of the same people, but some of the jobs and cities are different. Ask questions to find the differences. Circle them.

A: *Is Antonio Loren a model in your picture?*
B: *Yes, he is.*
A: *OK. That's the same. Is he from Rome?*
B: *No, he's from Milan. That's different.*

Family tree

A Draw your family tree. Include your family members, their names, and their ages.

My father César, 70	My mother Emilia, 68
My brother César, 47	Me Roberto, 43	My wife Claudia, 39
Our daughter Isabel, 10	Our son Iván, 8

My Family Tree

B **Pair work** Tell your partner about your family tree, but don't show it! Your partner draws it on another sheet of paper. Take turns.

A: *My grandfather is George. He's 72 years old. My grandmother is Anna.*
B: *How do you spell "Anna"?*
A: *A-N-N-A.*
B: *OK, thanks.*
A: *She's 68. Their kids are . . .*

C **Pair work** Compare your drawing with your partner's family tree. Are they the same?

Cleaning the closet

Pair work Look at Dean and Lucy's closet. What things are in their closet?

A: *What's that?*
B: *It's a dictionary. What's that?*
A: *It's a cell phone. Hey, what are these?*

What color?

Student A

A **Pair work** You and your partner have pictures of the same people, but some of their clothes are different colors. Describe the clothing to find the differences. Circle them.

Alice

Ben

Cindy

Drew

Ellen

Fred

Frank

> **A:** *In my picture, Alice's coat is blue and white.*
> **B:** *That's the same in mine. And her pants are gray.*
> **A:** *In my picture, her pants are green. That's different.*

B **Pair work** Cover the picture. What is the same? Answer with the information you remember.

> **A:** *Alice's coat is blue and white.*
> **B:** *Yes. And Ben's pants are . . .*

What color?

Student B

A Pair work You and your partner have pictures of the same people, but some of their clothes are different colors. Describe the clothing to find the differences. Circle them.

Alice · Ben · Cindy · Drew · Ellen · Fred · Frank

A: *In my picture, Alice's coat is blue and white.*
B: *That's the same in mine. And her pants are gray.*
A: *In my picture, her pants are green. That's different.*

B Pair work Cover the picture. What is the same? Answer with the information you remember.

A: *Alice's coat is blue and white.*
B: *Yes. And Ben's pants are . . .*

Car, train, bus, or bicycle?

A Look at the ways people get to work in Los Angeles.

How people in Los Angeles get to work

65%	drive alone
15%	drive with others
10%	take the bus
4%	walk
1%	ride a bicycle
5%	other

Source: www.fhwa.dot.gov/ctpp/jtw/jtw4.htm

Note: % = percent

B Pair work Guess the ways people get to work in New York City. Complete the chart with the numbers. Then check your answers on the bottom of page 134.

| 1% | 6% | 6% | 8% | 8% | 14% | 25% | 32% |

How people in New York City get to work

_____ %	drive alone
_____ %	drive with others
_____ %	take the bus
_____ %	walk
_____ %	take the subway
_____ %	take the train
_____ %	take a taxi
_____ %	other

Source: www.fhwa.dot.gov/ctpp/jtw/jtw4.htm

C Group work Guess the ways people get to work where *you* live. Rank them from 1 to 8.

_____ drive alone   _____ ride a bicycle   _____ take the bus   _____ walk

_____ drive with others _____ take a taxi   _____ take the train or subway _____ other

A: *I think number 1 is "take the train or subway."*
B: *I agree. I think number 2 is "drive alone."*

Routines

A Class activity Find classmates who do each thing. Write their names.

Find someone who . . .	Name	Find someone who . . .	Name
gets up before 6:00		sleeps a lot on weekends	
studies in the morning		walks to class	
takes a shower at night		has a red cell phone	
has coffee at home		studies on the bus	
reads every day		takes a bath in the morning	
goes to bed early		drives a sports car	
watches TV after midnight		doesn't have a dictionary	

take a shower

take a bath

drive a sports car

A: *Do you get up before 6:00, Donna?*
B: *No, I don't. I get up at 6:30.*
A: *How about you, Michael? Do you get up before 6:00?*
C: *Yes, I do.*

B Share your information.

A: *Michael gets up before 6:00.*
B: *And Angela gets up before 6:00. David studies in the morning.*

Answers to Keep talking! Unit 4 Lesson A, Part B (page 133): 25% drive alone, 6% drive with others, 14% take the bus, 8% walk, 32% take the subway, 8% take the train, 1% take a taxi, 6% other.

134 **Keep talking!**

On the computer

A Add two more questions about online activities to the chart.

Do you ever . . . ?	Name: _____
read people's blogs	
buy books online	
use online dictionaries	
search the Internet in English	
check the weather online	
get directions online	
check movie times online	

check the weather

get directions

check movie times

B **Pair work** Interview your partner. Complete the chart with his or her answers. Use adverbs of frequency.

A: *Naoko, do you ever read people's blogs?*
B: *Oh, yes. I often do. Do you?*
A: *I hardly ever do.*
B: *Do you ever . . . ?*

C **Pair work** Tell another classmate about your partner's answers.

A: *Naoko often reads people's blogs.*
B: *Sasha never does.*

Follow-up questions

A Add two follow-up questions about each topic to the charts.

Sports and games	Questions	Name: _____
	Do you ever play sports?	
	What do you play?	
	Who do you play with?	

Shopping	Questions	Name: _____
	Do you ever go shopping?	
	Where do you shop?	
	What do you buy there?	

Getting around	Questions	Name: _____
	Do you ever take the bus?	
	Why do you take the bus?	
	When do you take it?	

B Class activity Find a classmate who does each activity. Then ask the follow-up questions. Take notes.

A: *Do you ever play sports, Samantha.*
B: *Yes, I sometimes do.*
A: *What do you play?*
B: *I play tennis.*

C Share your information. What answers are popular in your class?

Job details

A Look at the picture for two minutes. Try to remember the people's names, jobs, and other information.

B **Pair work** Cover the picture. Ask the questions and answer with the information you remember.

- What does Pam do?
- Where does she work?
- Who does she work with?
- What does Paul do?
- How does Jane get to work?

- What does Tommy do?
- Where does Mei-li work?
- What does she do?
- What company does Mitch work for?
- What does Carla do?

> **A:** *What does Pam do?*
> **B:** *I think she's a waitress.*
> **A:** *Yes, I think so, too. Where does she work?*

C **Pair work** Ask and answer two more questions about the picture.

Start to finish

Group work Play the game. Put a small object on *Start*. Toss a coin.

 Move 1 space.

Heads

 Move 2 spaces.

Tails

Read the question. Can you do what it says? Take turns.

Yes. → Move ahead.　　　No. ← Move back.

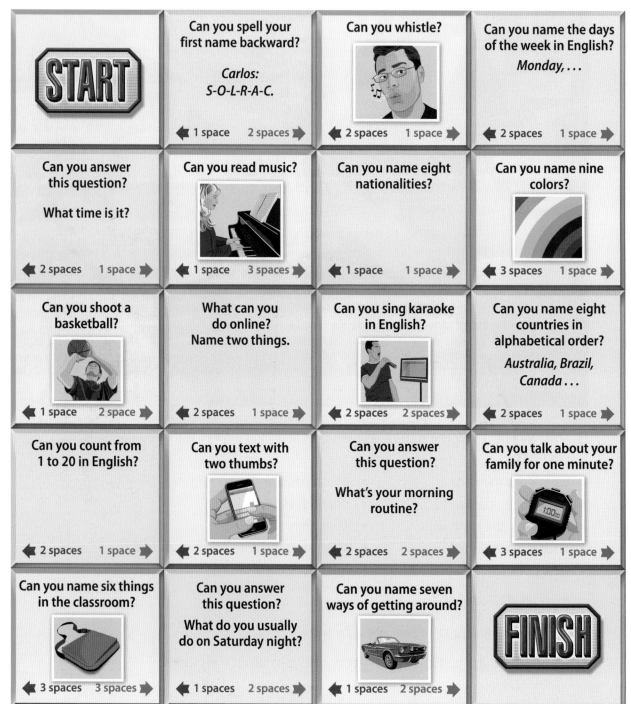

START

Can you spell your first name backward?

Carlos:
S-O-L-R-A-C.

◀ 1 space　　2 spaces ▶

Can you whistle?

◀ 2 spaces　　1 space ▶

Can you name the days of the week in English?

Monday, . . .

◀ 2 spaces　　1 space ▶

Can you answer this question?

What time is it?

◀ 2 spaces　　1 space ▶

Can you read music?

◀ 1 space　　3 spaces ▶

Can you name eight nationalities?

◀ 1 space　　1 space ▶

Can you name nine colors?

◀ 3 spaces　　1 space ▶

Can you shoot a basketball?

◀ 1 space　　2 space ▶

What can you do online? Name two things.

◀ 2 spaces　　1 space ▶

Can you sing karaoke in English?

◀ 2 spaces　　2 spaces ▶

Can you name eight countries in alphabetical order?

Australia, Brazil, Canada . . .

◀ 2 spaces　　1 space ▶

Can you count from 1 to 20 in English?

◀ 2 spaces　　1 space ▶

Can you text with two thumbs?

◀ 2 spaces　　1 space ▶

Can you answer this question?

What's your morning routine?

◀ 2 spaces　　2 spaces ▶

Can you talk about your family for one minute?

◀ 3 spaces　　1 space ▶

Can you name six things in the classroom?

◀ 3 spaces　　3 spaces ▶

Can you answer this question?

What do you usually do on Saturday night?

◀ 1 spaces　　2 spaces ▶

Can you name seven ways of getting around?

◀ 1 spaces　　2 spaces ▶

FINISH

Irregular verbs

Base form	Simple past
be	was, were
become	became
build	built
buy	bought
can	could
choose	chose
come	came
do	did
draw	drew
drink	drank
drive	drove
eat	ate
fall	fell
feel	felt
fly	flew
get	got
give	gave
go	went
hang	hung
have	had
hear	heard
hold	held
know	knew
leave	left

Base form	Simple past
lose	lost
make	made
meet	met
pay	paid
read	read
ride	rode
run	ran
say	said
see	saw
sell	sold
send	sent
sing	sang
sit	sat
sleep	slept
speak	spoke
spend	spent
stand	stood
swim	swam
take	took
teach	taught
think	thought
wear	wore
win	won
write	wrote

Credits

Illustration credits

Peter Ellis: 7, 16, 26; Tom Garrett: 25, 31, 35, 55, 130; John Goodwin: 4, 20, 129, 138 *(icons)*; Kim Johnson: 2, 3, 6, 10, 30, 40 *(bottom)*, 50, 59, 131, 132; Dean MacAdam: 41, 47, 60, 126, 127, 137; Michael Mantel: 39, 56; Garry Parsons: 36, 46 *(bottom)*, 53, 125, 134; Maria Rabinky: 15; Cristina Sampaio: 40 *(top)*, 57; Rob Schuster: 5, 27 *(bottom)*, 29, 46 *(top)*, 52, 138 *(board)*; Otto Steinenger: 27 *(top)*, 33

Photography credits

8 ©Media Bakery; 9 ©Media Bakery; 10 *(clockwise from top left)* ©Everett Collection; ©Everett Collection; ©Petite Poupee/Flickr; ©Frederick M. Brown/Getty Images; ©Kris Connor/Getty Images; ©Jeff Christensen/AP Wide World Photo; 12 *(clockwise from top left)* ©Elisabetta Villa/Getty Images; ©Everett Collection; ©Scott Gries/Getty Images; ©Kevin Mazur/Getty Images; ©Jamie McDonald/Getty Images; ©GV Cruz/Getty Images; 13 *(top to bottom)* ©Allstar Picture Library/Alamy; ©Allstar Picture Library/Alamy; ©Jon Kopaloff/Getty Images; ©Jon Kopaloff/Getty Images; 17 ©Photo Library; 18 ©Alamy; 22 *(clockwise from top left)* ©Media Bakery; ©Photo Library; ©Alamy; ©Derek Trask/Alamy; 23 *(top row, left to right)* ©Jenny Acheson/Getty Images; ©Media Bakery; ©Golden Pixels/Alamy; ©Michael Newman/Photo Edit; *(bottom)* ©Media Bakery; 26 *(top row, left to right)* ©Istock; ©Istock; ©Shutterstock; ©Adventure House; *(middle row, left to right)* ©Shutterstock; ©Media Bakery; ©Istock; ©Istock; *(bottom row, left to right)* ©Istock; ©Istock; ©Shutterstock; ©Dorling Kindersley/Getty Images; 28 *(top row, left to right)* ©Shutterstock; ©Dorling Kindersley/Getty Images; ©Shutterstock; ©David Young-Wolff/Photo Edit; *(bottom)* ©Frank Veronsky; 32 *(clockwise from top left)* ©Alamy; ©Lenscap/Alamy; ©Shutterstock; ©Shutterstock; ©Media Bakery; ©Urikiri-Shashin-Kan/Alamy; 33 *(clockwise from top left)* ©Dorling Kindersley/Getty Images; ©Istock; ©Istock; ©Shutterstock; ©Getty Images; ©Shutterstock; ©Shutterstock; ©Alamy; 34 *(clockwise from top left)* ©Shutterstock; ©Shutterstock; ©Helene Rogers/Alamy; ©Shutterstock; ©Shutterstock; ©Istock; 36 *(clockwise from top left)* ©Getty Images; ©Liu Xiaoyang/Alamy; ©Patrick Eden/Alamy; ©Tony Anderson/Getty Images; ©Alamy; ©Media Bakery; ©David Gee/Alamy; ©Alamy; 38 *(top two rows)* ©Shutterstock; *(bottom row)* ©Frank Veronsky; 39 ©Shutterstock; 42 *(top to bottom)* ©Shutterstock; ©Media Bakery; ©Istock; ©Media Bakery; ©Istock; ©Shutterstock; 44 *(all)* ©Shutterstock; 45 *(clockwise from top left)* ©Media Bakery; ©Media Bakery; ©Alex Segre/Alamy; ©Media Bakery; 46 *(middle row, left to right)* ©Camille Tokerud/Getty Images; ©Dreamstime; ©Media Bakery; 48 *(background store images)* ©Alamy; *(foreground people images)* ©Frank Veronsky; 49 *(all)* ©Shutterstock; 50 *(top row, left to right)* ©Photo Stock Israel/Alamy; ©Ryan McVay/Getty Images; ©Media Bakery; *(middle row, left to right)* ©Media Bakery; ©Alamy; ©Alamy; *(bottom row, left to right)* ©Robert Clayton/Alamy; ©David Sanger/Alamy; ©Perry Mastrovito/Getty Images; ©Alamy; ©Getty Images; 52 *(clockwise from top left)* ©Dreamstime; ©Norma Zuniga/Getty Images; ©David White/Alamy; ©Shutterstock; ©Alex Segre/Alamy; 53 *(left to right)* ©Kevin Foy/Alamy; ©Stephen Dunn/Getty Images; ©Alamy; ©Daniel Dempster/Alamy; 56 *(both)* ©Media Bakery; 58 *(top row)* ©Frank Veronsky; *(bottom row, left to right)* ©Golden Pixels/Alamy; ©Workbook Stock/Getty Images; ©Getty Images; ©Media Bakery; 60 *(clockwise from top left)* ©Media Bakery; ©Alamy; ©Alamy; ©Media Bakery; ©Media Bakery; ©Marmaduke St. John/Alamy; ©Media Bakery; ©Media Bakery; 62 *(top to bottom)* ©Media Bakery; ©Media Bakery; ©Getty Images; 63 *(left to right)* ©Media Bakery; ©China Photos/Getty Images; ©Media Bakery; 133 *(top to bottom)* ©Media Bakery; ©David Grossman/Alamy